TEACHINGS OF THE HINDU MYSTICS

Teachings

OF THE

HINDU
MYSTICS

Edited by
Andrew Harvey

SHAMBHALA
Boston & London
2001

SHAMBHALA PUBLICATIONS, INC.
Horticultural Hall
300 Massachusetts Avenue
Boston, Massachusetts 02115
www.shambhala.com

9 8 7 6 5 4 3 2 1

FIRST EDITION
Printed in the United States of America
♾ This edition is printed on acid-free paper that meets the
American National Standards Institute z39.48 Standard.
Distributed in the United States by Random House, Inc.,
and in Canada by Random House of Canada Ltd

LIBRARY OF CONGRESS CATALOGING-IN-PUBLICATION DATA

Teachings of the Hindu mystics/edited by Andrew Harvey.
   p. cm.
  Includes index.
  ISBN 1-57062-449-6 (pbk.)
    1. Mysticism—Hinduism.   2. Hinduism—Doctrines.
I. Harvey, Andrew, 1952–

BL1215.M9 S43   2001
294.5'422—dc21   2001032779

I would like to dedicate this book to my beloved friend Leila Hadley Luce, with whom I have shared countless hours of delight and a profound love for India.

Contents

Introduction

MAX MÜLLER, the pioneering Indologist of the nineteenth century, wrote, "We all come from the East and in going to the East everyone ought to feel that he is going to his 'old home' full of memories if only he could read them." Those words have a specially poignant meaning for me, since I was born in India of parents who themselves were born in India, spent the first nine years of my life there, and have returned as often as possible since, always to try and drink deeper from the still-living springs of its ancient passion and wisdom. The texts that I am offering in this anthology have been intimate companions for many years; India, in all its faces and powers, has been at the core of my life and search. India is, and always will be, the "old home" of my heart and of my soul.

One of the first things I learned as a child about "Hinduism" is that the word itself is inaccurate. An old Indian scholar friend of my parents explained to me patiently one morning that "Hindu" was originally a geographical rather than a religious term, used first in the Persian empire and then by the Greek soldiers and historians who followed Alexander as he swept across the world, for those who lived on the banks of the Indus River, in what is now the Punjab. "We Indians do not use this name," my friend said gently. "We call our religion the Sanatana Dharma—the 'Eternal Way.'" He spelled out the magical Sanskrit syllables slowly for me and then wrote them out in big letters in my red school notebook. Being an inquisitive seven year old, I asked, "Why do you call it the Eternal Way?" He looked a little startled and then almost whispered, "Because, my dear Andrew, it is eternal. The Sanatana Dharma, we believe, began when the universe was first unrolled out of the mind of God. It and creation began at exactly the same moment." Those words with their sense of a clear, majestic, changeless order thrilled me, and I repeated them to myself for years.

As a child, what I knew of this Sanatana Dharma was at once exotic and ordinary, homespun and picturesque. Hinduism for me was visits to temples where plump, smiling priests fed me sweets and introduced me to various gods swathed in brilliant yellow and purple silk; it was the garish shrines to Shiva and Vishnu by the side of the road, reeking of rancid butter, the festival of Holi with thousands of wild shriekers in the streets flinging fresh paint at each other, comic books with the stories of Krishna luridly fleshed out for children, the sound of temple bells echoing across moonlit fields, the tang of incense from our cook's tiny altar in the corner of his room. Once, as I was walking alone by the Jamuna River near our home, I saw an old holy man, a *sadhu* wrapped in a flame-orange robe, standing silently in prayer, his hands lifted in adoration to the rising sun; on his face I saw a look I had never seen in church, a look of still and incandescent devotion and tenderness; he seemed to be whispering to someone he knew very well and deeply. That afternoon I told my mother that I had seen a saint talking to God.

Later, when I came to discuss Hinduism with one of my

colleagues at All Souls College, Oxford—Robin Zaehner, the brilliant and eccentric translator of the Upanishads and Bhagavad Gita—I learned that in many ways "Hinduism" is nothing like what we normally think of as a religion. The Sanatana Dharma is a gallimaufry of the most extravagantly varied faiths, rituals, customs, and beliefs; Hinduism has no single dogmatic authority and, until very recently in its history, no "missionary zeal" to convert others, since it has never seen itself as the one true religion or the only hope of salvation. Zaehner was, when I knew him, a fervent Catholic convert, but he loved to exclaim, "If only the church had had the sense to allow so many different and seemingly contradictory approaches to God, how much saner its history would have been!"

It was this sublime ancient tolerance, Zaehner stressed often, that was the true proof of the wisdom and mature dignity of the Hindu tradition. "In the family of religions, Hinduism is the wise old all-knowing mother," he would say. "Its most sacred books, the Vedas, claim, 'Truth is one, but sages call it by different names.' If only Islam, and all the rest of the monotheistic 'book' religions, had learned that lesson, all the horror of history's religious wars could have been avoided. Which other religion has its God say, as Krishna does in the Bhagavad Gita, 'All paths lead to me'?" And here Zaehner would delight in repeating an anecdote he loved about a Protestant evangelical missionary trying to convert an old sage in Calcutta. "As you can imagine, the missionary pulled out all the stops. He wept and shuddered and shook and pleaded and implored and threatened hellfire and then evoked ecstatically all the joys of paradise. The old Indian sage listened quietly and, when he had finished, said, 'I accept wholeheartedly, dear honored sir, that Jesus Christ was a very great divine master whose life and teachings are of permanent sacred value to humanity. But the Buddha was also such a divine master, and so, I might add, was my dear Swami, Sri Ramakrishna. Why would God, after all, be so mean as to give humanity only one divine master and that one only for the white people?' At that, the missionary flung up his hands in horror and fled the room."

The sage in Zaehner's story was, it seems, a disciple of the great nineteenth-century Indian saint Ramakrishna and it was Zaehner, in fact, who first read to me the following passage from *The Gospel of Ramakrishna* that enshrines the Sanatana Dharma's "motherly" embrace of all ways to the Divine:

> God has made different religions to suit different aspirations, times and countries. All doctrines are only so many paths; but a path is by no means God himself. Indeed we can reach God if we follow any of the paths with whole-hearted devotion. One may eat a cake with icing either straight or sidewise. It will taste sweet either way.
>
> As we can ascend to the top of a house by ladder or bamboo or a staircase or a rope, so diverse are the ways to approach God and every religion shows one of these ways.
>
> People partition off their lands by means of boundaries, but no one can partition off the all-embracing sky overhead. The indivisible sky surrounds all and includes all. So people in ignorance say, "My religion

is the only one, my religion is the best." But when the heart is illumined by true knowledge it knows that above all of these sects and sectarians presides the one indivisible eternal all-knowing bliss.

As a mother, in nursing her sick children, gives rice and curry to one, and sago and arrowroot to another, and bread and butter to a third, so the Lord has laid out different paths for different people.

For all its tolerance and variety of faiths and beliefs, however, there *are* certain essential beliefs and attitudes of spirit that bind together all those we call "Hindus." Nearly all religious Hindus share a profound faith in rebirth and karma, in the cyclical nature of time, in the transcendent and immanent Presence of the Divine, in the ultimately delusory and unsatisfactory nature of a life lived in ignorance of eternal truth, and in the supreme value of *moksha,* or liberation from all inner and outer limitations. Moreover, the different schools of Hinduism—while they may disagree even within themselves on such seemingly crucial issues as the nature of absolute reality, the status of the individual self, and the reality of the world—all derive their authority from the most ancient body of texts, the Vedas, which contain not only the great hymns of the Rig Veda (which begin my anthology) but also the Upanishads, the multifaceted core of Indian mysticism. While there is no one "exclusive" dogmatic Hindu tradition, then, there is, very definitely, a spirit of inquiry and of revelation that is so consistent that we find one of the greatest of modern Hindu mystics, Ramana Maharshi, speaking in ways and with images that echo exactly the terminology of the anonymous seers who wrote down the Upanishads more than two thousand years before him. It is this consistency that gives the Hindu mystical tradition its timeless purity, weight, and grandeur. It is as if one eternal voice is speaking in and through a myriad different voices tirelessly exploring different registers of its own majestic range, as if all the tradition's poems and meditations and philosophical texts are, as Zaehner once said to me, "different-shaped peaks in one vast, grand, interconnected mountain chain, like the Himalayas."

What I have wanted to do in this anthology is to honor this consistency of vision and to present it in the way most relevant to all seekers on all paths today, and most pertinent to the dangers and challenges facing our world. I wanted to create an anthology that would—in the spirit of the Gita and Ramakrishna—inspire all readers, whatever their religious background or lack of it, to plunge into the uncovering of their eternal nature and then enact its sacred laws in loving action in the world. As it is written in the Svetashvatara Upanishad, "What use are the scriptures to anyone who knows not the source from which they come?" And as the Yoga Vasishtha warns us, "If you conceptualize these teachings for your intellectual entertainment and do not let them act in your life, you will stumble and fall like a blind person." For all its metaphysical loftiness and joy in speculation, the Hindu mystical tradition, like all true mystical traditions, is essentially practical, concerned with teaching, inspiring, and guiding authentic transformation. Whatever path you are on, then, use these texts not as intellectual puzzles but as signs of your essential splendor; pray, meditate, and serve others so that the wordless truth behind these truths can be revealed to you in your own life.

What, then, is the core truth of the Hindu tradition? It is the truth of the mystery of a Spirit that pervades, creates, and transcends all things and of each soul's conscious identity with it beyond space and time. In the Upanishads, this all-pervading, all-creating, all-transcending Spirit is named Brahman. In parts of the earlier Vedas, Brahman—from the Sanskrit *br*, to "become" or "breathe," and *brih*, "to be great"—means "that which is powerful and great" and most often refers to the force inherent in sacred hymns and sacrifices. In the Upanishads this concept widens, and Brahman becomes the Presence underlying, creating, and sustaining all of existence. For the Upanishads and all the later teachings rooted in them, every human being is naturally one with Brahman in his or her Atman, his or her "soul" or "indwelling core of divine consciousness." The aim of human life and the source of liberation from all the chains of life and death is to know, from inmost experience, the Atman's identity with Brahman and to live the calm, fearless, selflessly loving life that radiates from this knowledge.

There was a danger inherent in the tradition's celebration of the transcendent Brahman and of freedom from the world—the danger of what might be called an "addiction to transcendence" and a corresponding subtle but devastating devaluation of creation and life as "unreal." Many developments of the Hindu tradition did not escape this danger, but it is important to recognize that it was recognized and dealt with at the very beginning of the tradition's unfolding—both in the Vedas, with their celebration of the glory of the creation, and in the crucial and exalted statement of the necessity of "sacred balance" between immanence and transcendence, Being and Becoming, contemplative awareness and just action, that we discover in the Isha Upanishad:

> In dark night live those for whom
> The world without alone is real; in night
> Darker still, for whom the world within
> Alone is real. The first leads to a life
> Of action, the second to a life of meditation.
> But those who combine action with meditation
> Cross the sea of death through action
> And enter into immortality
> Through the practice of meditation.
> So have we heard from the wise.

It was this mature and practical sacred balance between transcendence and immanence, meditation and service, that the Bhagavad Gita, composed several centuries after the Upanishads, brought to a marvelous depth of richness in its central vision of "selfless action." In the Gita, Lord Krishna teaches his disciple Arjuna the timeless secret of an action inspired by divine will, wisdom, love, and knowledge, performed for its own sake and without attachment to results: only such action, Krishna tells Arjuna, can free a person from the chains of karma and also allow the Divine to use him or her for Its own purpose without any interference of the false self and so secure the triumph of sacred law and justice in history. Many modern mystics—I am one of them—believe that it is such a vision of "selfless action" that can most richly inspire the kind of "mystical activism" that is necessary in all arenas if we are going to preserve the planet. Activism without mystical inspiration and the strength, stamina, and passion that spring from divine love and divine knowledge will inevitably cause us to grow jaded and despairing in the bitter fierce world of reality; mysticism without a commitment to enacting justice and truth in life will degenerate into what Gandhi called "the higher narcissism" and what Vivekananda derided as "heartless escapism masquerading as illumination." Krishna's revelation to Arjuna, then, of a middle way that fuses the deepest insights of contemplation with tireless service of the Divine in the Real may well hold the secret to our survival as a race, and to the survival of the natural world.

Lord Krishna's teaching in the Bhagavad Gita also suggests another holy secret that has inspired some of the greatest mystics of the Hindu tradition. Simply stated, the human being only achieves union with God in all of His aspects through a fusion of contemplation and action. God is after all both Eternal Being *and* Eternal Becoming; in contemplative knowledge of our eternal identity with Brahman, we rest in God's Being, like a drop of water in the all-surrounding ocean; in enacting the divine will selflessly, we participate in the transforming activity of God, in what a great mystic of another tradition, Rumi, called "God's perpetual massive resurrection." Both aspects of the Godhead, then, are open to us to taste, savor, celebrate, and enshrine, and life itself is the dancing ground of this divine human dance of opposites; the site of a perpetually evolving Sacred Marriage between matter and spirit whose potential possibilities and glories are boundless. What could a humanity attuned intimately to the Divine and selflessly transparent to Its Will not achieve?

The Hindu tradition provides exquisite, firm guidance toward this attunement because it has always recognized that different temperaments take different paths into the Sacred Marriage. It has not only recognized the validity of other religions but has also acknowledged within itself a variety of paths. Of these, the four main ways to *yoga* (union with God) are *jnana yoga*, the path to the transcendent through direct intuitive knowledge; *bhakti yoga*, which focuses the powers of imagination and passion on a path of devotion, usually to a personal God; *raja yoga*, the path of "royal (*raj*) integration" through psychophysical exercises; and *karma yoga*, the path of works and action dedicated selflessly to the Supreme. None of these yogas excludes the practice of any of the others. Each temperament, however, finds in one or another of the paths its own door into that experience of the living Presence most natural to it; and as this experience deepens, the chosen path opens to the realization of all the other paths and gradually fuses with them to birth a mature divine human being. No other mystical tradition has had so broad and wise and all-embracing a vision of the different aspects and faces of the path. Robin Zaehner used to say, "If anyone feels excluded from the Hindu embrace it is by his or her own perverse choice."

In this anthology, I have chosen to emphasize—but by no means exclusively—the sacred texts devoted to *bhakti yoga*, the yoga of devotion or adoration. Sri Ramakrishna never tired of repeating that *bhakti yoga* is the path suited to the most people, the easiest to keep performing in the heart of the world, and the yoga most apt for this dark age, when religious culture is everywhere in decline and the exigencies of work make the time for more elaborate spiritual exercises hard to secure. *Bhakti yoga*, of course, opens on to all the other yogas: As Ramakrishna said, "The more you love, the more you know; the more you love and know, the more deeply you plunge into sacred action born from love and knowledge."

The great *bhakti* river of Hindu mysticism has its origins in the Vedas where many gods—all of them different aspects of the One—are celebrated. In its more identifiable modern form, however, it began around the fourth century BCE, when several religious groups made their appearance worshiping a Supreme God in His personal aspect as Vasudeva, Narayana, or Hari (later all three would be identified with Vishnu). During the next two thousand years, other streams of devotion—to Shiva, God of Destruction and Renewal; to the Goddess in all Her different forms and names; and to Krishna (an embodiment of Vishnu whose devotion began to flourish in the sixth century)—also joined this vast river.

It is vital to remember, however, that despite this plurality of divine names and forms and objects of adoration, Hinduism is not polytheistic; the different "gods" each represent different aspects of the Supreme. As Huston Smith writes in his *World Religions*: "It is obtuse to confuse Hinduism's images with idolatry and their multiplicity with polytheism. They are runways from which the sense-laden human spirit can rise for its 'flight of the alone to the Alone.'"

In traditional Hindu metaphysics, Brahman is recognized as having two faces: the Nirguna Brahman of many of the earliest Upanishads—the Self without qualities and beyond all concepts and form—and Saguna Brahman, the Spirit as Form or forms, with qualities that can be approached and adored. In practice, many Hindu mystics moved between these two aspects of the Absolute with natural delight; even so austere a lover of the Nirguna Brahman as Shankara, the great philosopher of nondual Vedanta, also wrote ecstatic devotional hymns to the Saguna Brahman as Shiva or the Divine Mother. And Ramakrishna, in the course of a single discourse, can veer between the formless absolute and "the Mother" and back again, knowing their identity in the Mystery that transcends all names and concepts. The face the Divine wears in the *bhakti* tradition always has the majesty of the Formless in and behind it; when Baby Krishna's foster mother, Yashoda, looks into his mouth after scolding him for eating mud, she sees the whole universe ablaze in divine fire.

The glory of the *bhakti* tradition—in Mirabai's hymns to Krishna, as in Mahadeviyakka's to Shiva and Ramprasad's to the Mother—lies in its fierce emotional courage and passion. As the French thinker Simone Weil remarked to an atheist philosopher who was mocking the erotic language of certain Christian mystics and of the biblical Song of Songs: "The language of love belongs to mystics by right; other kinds of lovers merely borrow it." That God is Love—eternal, boundless, fiery ecstatic Love—is known and experienced by mystics of all traditions: It is this Love that is the Energy and Force that creates, and sustains all things and worlds.

In the *bhakti* tradition the "language of love" that such a Love inevitably arouses in its passionate devotees is explored in all its nuances of coquetry, agony, longing, and sometimes even molten rage at divine "cruelty." In shamelessly exposing all possible responses to the Divine—imaged as friend, mentor, mother, child, and especially lover—the *bhakti* tradition helps all seekers on all paths to dedicate the full range, passion, and power of their emotions to God, and so enter into a nakedly intense personal relationship with the Divine. Mirabai, Mahadeviyakka, Ramprasad, and the other great poets of the *bhakti* tradition bring their entire tumultuous complex selves to the encounter with the Beloved, censoring nothing and leaving out no part of their being; their huge pains and ecstasies challenge us to expose ourselves also to the irradiation of Love and its often ferocious alchemy.

For those who find the Nirguna Brahman too cold an object to pursue, adoring God-in-Form is a marvelously powerful way of keeping the whole being in the crucible of transformation until all of its ignorance and folly are burned away and a new being is ultimately forged in gold from the ashes of the old. As its crowning grace, adoration reveals the whole of creation as a nondual interdependent dancing-ground of Love; as the Baul poet Fikirchand sings so movingly:

> If I look at the clouds in the sky,
> I see His beauty afloat;
> And I see him walk on the stars
> Blazing my heart.

This revelation of all beings, things, and events, being swept up in an infinite, interconnected, nondual Dance of Bliss–consciousness sources the second great stream of

Hindu mysticism I have chosen to celebrate in this anthology—that of the Tantric tradition. The word *Tantra* is derived from the Sanskrit *tan*, to stretch and expand; "Tantric" signifies that by which knowledge and consciousness are stretched and expanded so that the full sublime passion and power and wisdom of the Dance can infuse and illumine them. The Tantric tradition is reflected in Jnaneshwar's "Hymn to Self-Awareness," the Devi Gita, Kabir, the songs of the mystic minstrels known as the Bauls, and the excerpts from the works of Ramakrishna and Aurobindo.

This magnificent tradition first made its literary appearance toward the middle of the first millennium CE. From the beginning, it celebrated, with enormous fervor, the feminine aspect of the Godhead, the Shakti, the fire-energy that streams from the source to engender the creation and live in it. By honoring the Shakti, the Tantric devotee would make him- or herself open to Her transforming power and to the all-healing revelation of Her presence in and as all things and beings. The great Tantric formula (fundamental also to Mahayana Buddhism) is "*Samsara* equals *nirvana*"—which reveals that the world and the creation in all their holy particulars are coessential with the transcendent Being-Consciousness-Bliss. Everything, in its inherent bliss-nature, is divine and holy; there is nothing but God in us and around us at all times. For the Tantric schools, *moksha*, or liberation, does not come from renouncing reality, leaving the world, or killing one's natural desires. Rather true freedom arises naturally and sumptuously when what has been categorized as the "lower" reality is seen and known as contained within and always melting into the "higher," and when the "higher" is constantly invoked to penetrate and transfigure the "lower" at ever-greater depths of power, presence, and rapture. To the Tantric mystic, the entire universe is the site of a constantly consummated, explosively and boundlessly fertile Sacred Marriage between the transcendent Source and His immanent Shakti, between the self and the Self, matter and spirit. For the Tantric, the aim of human existence is to participate in this dynamic marriage, and to make all aspects of life radiant with its holy truth and joy.

Georg Feuerstein writes in *The Yoga Tradition*: "It is important to realize that the Tantra revolution was not the product of mere philosophical speculation. Though connected with an immense architecture of old and new concepts and doctrines, Tantrism is intensely practical. . . . Historically, Tantra can be understood as a dialectical response to the often abstract approach of Advaita Vedanta, which was and still is the dominant philosophy of the Hindu elite. Tantra was a grassroots movement, and many if not most of its early protagonists hailed from the castes at the bottom of the social pyramid of India—fishermen, weavers, hunters, street vendors, washerwomen. They were responding to a widely felt need for more practical orientation that would integrate the lofty metaphysical ideals of non-dualism with down-to-earth procedures for living a sanctified life." (p. 456)

Of all the different streams of the Hindi mystical tradition, it is, I believe, the Tantric that offers most to us today. At a time when the natural world is itself in danger, the last thing the human race needs are mystical theologies addicted to transcendence. It is this addiction to otherworldliness, to a vision of freedom or "heaven" that lies outside the body and matter and time that has, in all the major religions, abetted our coma of denial about our connection to our bodies and the world around us, a denial that is now lethally abetting our destruction of the environment. The Tantric vision of a *samsara* that is also *nirvana*, of an earth that is also heaven, of a body ensouled and a soul embodied, can help us live in the creation as in a temple, transfigure banal desire into holy celebration, and love our lives with sacred passion and so gather our powers to protect and honor the lives of all beings with courage and wisdom. Only such a passion, courage, and wisdom—and the hope born from them of a divine life in an increasingly divinized world—can give us now the fire and the strength to save our world from disaster. The great German poet Hölderlin wrote at the beginning of the nineteenth century that "at the time of greatest danger, salvation arises." In our contemporary danger, "salvation" is a vision of the world, creation, and our lives as inherently blessed and potentially divinely empowered, just, impassioned, and creative. From such a vision—that of Tantra at its highest and richest— can spring astonishing powers of sacrifice and invention, stamina and hope. If we are going to find the strength as a race to band together to save the planet, it will be in the name of a world and a creation seen and known as holy, not "unreal"; as the sacred ground on and in which miracles of divine human evolution can still unfold, if we can only honor its laws.

The key to an integration of the Tantric vision into every aspect of our lives and actions is, as I have already hinted, an exaltation and adoration of the Sacred Feminine in all its forms and powers. It is this exaltation and adoration of the Mother aspect of God, the Tantric mystics assure us, that will restore to our deepest understanding the divinity of creation and enable us to flood our lives with sacred tenderness, joy, and power. Kabir wrote, "The formless Absolute is my Father, and God with form is my Mother"; for Jnaneshwar too, as his glorious hymn to Shiva and Shakti proclaims, the universe and every human being are the sites of a marriage between Shiva and Shakti. There can be no marriage, however, without a Bride. In nearly all the major mystical systems, the Sacred Feminine has been lost or suppressed: it is this drastic loss and suppression that has prevented the birth on a large scale of a divine humanity. Without conscious awareness of the Sacred Feminine, of the feminine as sacred, the marriage—of immanence and transcendence, heart and mind, body and soul, masculine and feminine powers—that is meant to take place at the core of every human being to birth him or her into the authentic divine human reality, fully empowered, and fully creative in all arenas of life, simply cannot take place.

Perhaps the supreme gift of Hinduism to the world is that its Tantric traditions have kept the truth of the splendor, majesty, and power of the Bride vibrant and alive in all her unbridled fullness. Worshiping Her as Devi, Ambika, Durga, Lakshmi, or Kali, the Hindu Tantric mystics have known how to adore Her both as Queen of Transcendence *and* Earth Mother, and love Her both in Her terrifying, life-devouring aspects and as infinitely benign and tender. Their triumph has been not to water down or domesticate or "masculinize" the Mother but to allow Her to be Her full, gorgeous, wild, unpredictable, menacing, miraculous self, in all Her paradoxes and seeming contradictions, and to find the way to connect directly with Her all-transforming power through an embrace of Her in an adoration without conditions.

Ramakrishna described the Mother as a "spider who has spun the universe out of her entrails and gone to live herself in each shining strand of her Web." In his last years he had a vision of Her, at once magnificent and appalling, as a beautiful pregnant woman arising out of the waves of the Ganges, birthing her child on the shore, tearing it to pieces, smiling, and then, with blood all over her face and mouth, walking serenely back into the waves of the river to merge with them. Ramakrishna's abandoned and unconditional love of the Mother gave him the heart-power to embrace Her in *all* of her moods and facets, as Destroyer as well as Preserver, and so to share in Her timeless Bliss-dance, beyond space and time and matter and beyond all conventional—or convenient—religious or moral categories. Such an unconditional embrace of the Mother-aspect of the Godhead as "naked Reality" in its extremes of life and death, "good" and "evil," horror and Bliss leads to the highest nondual realization, a realization that sees, knows, feels, exalts the Divine in all things and events, with a sublime outrageous fearlessness, in a rapture of freedom. This ultimate realization, Ramakrishna made clear, is always the gift of the Mother, for only the force and love of the Mother can forever explode and rubble all possible distinctions between "here" and "there," "eternity" and "time," "Body" and "Soul" and so finally birth her divine human child into deathless Presence, alive with the Mother's own miraculous power of healing and creativity. And in his extraordinary life, Ramakrishna gave us sign after sign that he had truly become her child, the founder-father-mother of a whole new world of children waiting to be born.

This Tantric embrace of all the powers and aspects of the Divine Mother and of the miraculous transformations it makes possible infuses the extraordinary evolutionary vision of the greatest mystical philosopher of Hinduism, and perhaps of all human history: Sri Aurobindo. In his astounding series of books, from the *Foundation of Indian Culture* to *The Synthesis of Yoga* and *The Life Divine*, Aurobindo gathers masterfully together all the various strands of the Hindu mystical tradition, all the deepest truths of the Upanishadic, *bhakti*, and Tantric traditions, and fuses them at diamond-pure heat with the most advanced Western understanding of historical evolution and progress. Out of this fusion of the deepest, broadest, and richest knowledge of both "sides" of the world's "mind" arises what many people consider to be the map of the possible future of humanity—a future that could see the whole of earth-life transfigured consciously by the descending power of the Divine Mother and of that initiatory "supramental" light-force that is in Her gift and control.

Other mystical systems have had a vision of what might be called "radiant apocalypse." Gregory of Nyssa and other Christian mystics envisaged all of the creation being transfigured by divine grace into the Pleroma, the divine fullness or glory, and Mahayana masters in Tibet and China taught and wrote about the coming reign of Shambhala, a heavenly kingdom on earth that would spread its rays of peace, health, and illumination everywhere. No one, however, in human history has had so precise a vision of transfiguration as Aurobindo; to call it a vision, in fact, is to limit its significance, for it was a living "scientific" experience he underwent himself and described in meticulous detail up until his death, leaving behind, in his letters especially, very direct practical advice for anyone who wanted, like him, to be a pioneer of the Mother's New Reality.

It is not a coincidence, I believe, that such an all-comprehensive, both dazzlingly inspired and dazzlingly lucid vision of the evolutionary possibilities of humanity, should have arisen at the very moment during the first two world wars when the future of humanity was first revealed as dangerously fragile. Just as the battles of the Somme and Marne and later the rise of Fascism and the explosion of the atom bomb at Hiroshima were ushering in our age of tragic despair and violence, so, in Aurobindo, the genius of the Hindu mystical tradition was bringing to birth one final, believable, potentially all-transforming vision of the possible human future. Mystics of all traditions know the sacred, mysterious law by which the darkest midnights birth the most resplendent suns; the annihilation of all old forms with their attendant institutions and illusions is sometimes necessary before the full glory and outrageousness of the new can flash out. One world is clearly dying in agony around us; another is trying to rise, phoenix-like, from its ashes.

Although Aurobindo knew that his vision of a new gnostic human race was real and possible because he was living it, he also knew that its birth on a large enough scale to influence the course of history was far from inevitable, however great the divine powers gathered by the Mother to help it. Divine lights and initiations, dark and brilliant, may stream toward us, but the future will always depend on how profoundly receptive we are to them and how radical and brave we are in enacting the miraculous possibilities they open up to us.

Time is running out. As Georg Trakl, the great German prophet-poet, wrote in an unnamed poem during the First World War, "The hands of the clock are climbing towards midnight." Will the extreme danger of our time lead to Birth or Apocalypse, to a new, mystically inspired, universal humanity or our death and the death of most of nature? In our time, the Divine stands before us, nakedly offering us two mirrors in which we can see two contrasting destinies. One is a black mirror in which the last tree of the last forest is being burned down as the last whales and dolphins die in finally polluted seas and the entire planet becomes, in the environmentalist David Brower's words, "a vast stinking hospital of the dead and dying." The other is a golden mirror, in which we can also see clearly, if we dare to look at what our inner glory and divine power and beauty could create with divine grace, wisdom, and a transfigured world, a mirror of Love and Justice, a place where the Sacred Marriage becomes real in all its holy laws and potentials in all arts and sciences and institutions and technologies. It is our tragedy and our magnificence that both destinies should now be possible and within our grasp.

Which of our fates will we choose? No one knows, and all prophecies in a time like ours are straws thrown into a whirlwind. I have chosen the world I see clearly in the golden mirror. And in my own struggle to realize its laws within my own heart, mind, body, and soul, I find that the testimony of the Hindu mystical tradition to the divinity within us all and the powers that stream from that divinity is of priceless practical usefulness and inspiration. On dark days, I try to remember what Aurobindo writes in one of his last letters: "In the way that one treads with the greater Light above, even every difficulty gives its help and Night itself carries in it the burden of the Light that has to be."

Teachings of the Hindu Mystics

In the Beginning Love Arose

At first was neither Being nor Nonbeing.
There was not air nor yet sky beyond.
What was its wrapping? Where? In whose protection?
Was Water there, unfathomable and deep?

There was no death then, nor yet deathlessness;
of night or day there was not any sign.
The One breathed without breath, by its own impulse.
Other than that was nothing else at all.

Darkness was there, all wrapped around by darkness,
and all was Water indiscriminate. Then
that which was hidden by the Void, that One, emerging,
stirring, through power of Ardor, came to be.

In the beginning Love arose,
which was the primal germ cell of the mind.
The Seers, searching in their hearts with wisdom,
discovered the connection of Being in Nonbeing.

A crosswise line cut Being from Nonbeing.
What was described above it, what below?
Bearers of seed there were and mighty forces,
thrust from below and forward move above.

Who really knows? Who can presume to tell it?
Whence was it born? Whence issued this creation?

Even the Gods came after its emergence.
Then who can tell from whence it came to be?

That out of which creation has arisen,
whether it held it firm or it did not,
He who surveys it in the highest heaven,
He surely knows—or maybe He does not!

—*Rig Veda 10.129*

Creative Fervor

From blazing Ardor Cosmic Order came
and Truth; from thence was born the obscure night;
from thence the Ocean with its billowing waves.

From Ocean with its waves was born the year
which marshals the succession of nights and days,
controlling everything that blinks the eye.

Then, as before, did the creator fashion
the Sun and Moon, the heaven and the Earth,
the atmosphere and the domain of light.

In the beginning arose the Golden Germ:
he was, as soon as born, the Lord of Being,
sustainer of the Earth and of this Heaven.
What God shall we adore with our oblation?

He who bestows life-force and hardy vigor,
whose ordinances even the Gods obey,
whose shadow is immortal life—and death—
What God shall we adore with our oblation?

Who by his grandeur has emerged sole sovereign
of every living thing that breathes and slumbers,
he who is Lord of man and four-legged creatures—
What God shall we adore with our oblation? . . .

Toward him, trembling, the embattled forces,
riveted by his glory, direct their gaze.
Through him the risen sun sheds forth its light.
What God shall we adore with our oblation?

When came the mighty Waters, bringing with them
the universal Germ, whence sprang the Fire,
thence leapt the God's One Spirit into being.
What God shall we adore with our oblation? . . .

O Lord of creatures, Father of all beings,
you alone pervade all that has come to birth.
Grant us our heart's desire for which we pray.
May we become the lords of many treasures!

—*Rig Veda 10.190*

The Mighty Earth

THE MIGHTY burden of the mountains' bulk
rests, Earth, upon your shoulders; rich in torrents,
you germinate the seed with quickening power.

Our hymns of praise resounding now invoke you,
O far-flung Earth, the bright one.
Like a neighing steed you drive abroad your storm clouds.

You in your sturdy strength hold fast the forests,
clamping the trees all firmly to the ground,
when rains and lightning issue from your clouds.

High Truth, unyielding Order, Consecration,
Ardor and Prayer and Holy Ritual
uphold the Earth; may she, the ruling Mistress
of what has been and what will come to be,
for us spread wide a limitless domain.

Impart to us those vitalizing forces
that come, O Earth, from deep within your body,
your central point, your navel; purify us wholly.
The Earth is mother; I am son of Earth.
The Rain-giver is my father; may he shower on us
    blessings! . . .

Instill in me abundantly that fragrance,
O Mother Earth, which emanates from you

and from your plants and waters, that sweet perfume
that all celestial beings are wont to emit,
and let no enemy ever wish us ill! . . .

Peaceful and fragrant, gracious to the touch,
may Earth, swollen with milk, her breasts overflowing,
grant me her blessing together with her milk! . . .

—Rig Veda 5.84

The Man

A THOUSAND-HEADED is the Man
with a thousand eyes, a thousand feet;
encompassing the Earth all sides,
he exceeded it by ten fingers' breadth.

The Man, indeed, is this All,
what has been and what is to be,
the Lord of the immortal spheres
which he surpasses by consuming food.

Such is the measure of his might,
and greater still than this is Man.
All beings are a fourth of him,
three fourths are the immortal in heaven.

Three-fourths of Man ascended high,
one-fourth took birth again down here.
From this he spread in all directions
into animate and inanimate things.

From him the Shining one was born;
from this Shining one Man again took birth.
As soon as born, he extended himself
all over the Earth both behind and before.

Using the Man as their oblation,
the Gods performed the sacrifice.

Spring served them for the clarified butter,
Summer for the fuel, and Autumn for the offering.

This evolved Man, then first born,
they besprinkled on the sacred grass.
With him the Gods performed the sacrifice,
as did also the heavenly beings and seers.

From this sacrifice, fully accomplished,
was gathered curd mixed with butter.
Thence came the creatures of the air,
beasts of the forest and those of the village.

From this sacrifice, fully accomplished,
were born the hymns and the melodies;
from this were born the various meters;
from this were born the sacrificial formulas.

From this were horses born, all creatures
such as have teeth in either jaw;
from this were born the breeds of cattle;
from this were born sheep and goats.

When they divided up the Man,
into how many parts did they divide him?
What did his mouth become? What his arms?
What are his legs called? What his feet?

His mouth became the brahmin; his arms
became the warrior-prince, his legs

the common man who plies his trade;
the lowly serf was born from his feet.

The Moon was born from his mind;
the Sun came into being from his eye;
from his mouth came Indra and Agni,
while from his breath the Wind was born.

From his navel issued the Air;
from his head unfurled the Sky,
the Earth from his feet, from his ear the four directions.
Thus have the worlds been organized.

Seven were the sticks of the enclosure,
thrice seven the fuel sticks were made,
when the Gods, performing the sacrifice,
bound the Man as the victim.

With the sacrifice the Gods sacrificed to the sacrifice.
Those were the first established rites.
These powers ascended up to heaven
where dwell the ancient Gods and other beings.

—*Rig Veda 10.90*

Shanti

PEACEFUL BE HEAVEN, peaceful the earth,
  peaceful the broad space between.
Peaceful for us be the running waters,
  peaceful the plants and herbs!
Peaceful to us be the signs of the future,
  peaceful what is done and undone,
peaceful to us be what is and what will be.
  May all to us be gracious!

This supreme Goddess, Word, inspired by Brahman,
  by which the awe-inspiring is created,
    through her to us be peace!

This supreme Spirit, inspired by Brahman,
  by which the awe-inspiring is created,
    through it to us be peace!

These five sense organs, with the mind as the sixth,
  within my heart, inspired by Brahman,
    by which the awe-inspiring is created,
      through them to us be peace!

Peace be to earth and to airy spaces!
Peace be to heaven, peace to the waters,
peace to the plants and peace to the trees!
May all the Gods grant to me peace!
By this invocation of peace may peace be diffused!

By this invocation of peace may peace bring peace!
With this peace the dreadful I now appease,
with this peace the cruel I now appease,
with this peace all evil I now appease,
so that peace may prevail, happiness prevail!
May everything for us be peaceful!

To the heavens be peace, to the sky and the earth,
to the waters be peace, to plants and all trees,
to the Gods be peace, to Brahman be peace,
to all men be peace, again and again
—peace also to me!

—*Atharva Veda 19.9*

Brahman Is Joy

ONCE BHRIGU VARUNI went to his father, Varuna, and said: "Father, explain to me the mystery of Brahman."

Then his father spoke to him of the food of the earth, of the breath of life, of the one who sees, of the one who hears, of the mind that knows, and of the one who speaks. And he further said to him: "Seek to know him from whom all beings have come, by whom they all live, and unto whom they all return. He is Brahman."

So Bhrigu went and practiced *tapas*, spiritual prayer. Then he thought that Brahman was the food of the earth: for from the earth all beings have come, by food of the earth they all live, and unto the earth they all return.

After this he went again to his father, Varuna, and said: "Father, explain further to me the mystery of Brahman." To him his father answered: "Seek to know Brahman by *tapas*, by prayer, because Brahman is prayer."

So Bhrigu went and practiced *tapas*, spiritual prayer. Then he thought that Brahman was life: for from life all beings have come, by life they all live, and unto life they all return.

After this he went again to his father, Varuna, and said: "Father, explain further to me the mystery of Brahman." To him his father answered: "Seek to know Brahman by *tapas*, by prayer, because Brahman is prayer."

So Bhrigu went and practiced *tapas*, spiritual prayer. Then he thought that Brahman was mind: for from mind all beings have come, by mind they all live, and unto mind they all return.

After this he went again to his father, Varuna, and said: "Father, explain further to me the mystery of Brahman." To him his father answered: "Seek to know Brahman by *tapas*, by prayer, because Brahman is prayer."

So Bhrigu went and practiced *tapas*, spiritual prayer. Then he thought that Brahman was reason: for from reason all beings have come, by reason they all live, and unto reason they all return.

He went again to his father, asked the same question, and received the same answer.

So Bhrigu went and practiced *tapas*, spiritual prayer. Then he thought that Brahman was joy: for *from joy all beings have come, by joy they all live, and unto joy they all return.*

This was the vision of Bhrigu Varuni which came from the highest; and he who sees this vision lives in the Highest.

—*From the Taittiriya Upanishad*

The Isha Upanishad

THE LORD is enshrined in the hearts of all.
The Lord is the supreme Reality.
Rejoice in him through renunciation.
Covet nothing. All belongs to the Lord.
Thus working may you live a hundred years.
Thus alone will you work in real freedom.

Those who deny the Self are born again
Blind to the Self, enveloped in darkness,
Utterly devoid of love for the Lord.

The Self is one. Ever still, the Self is
Swifter than thought, swifter than the senses.
Though motionless, he outruns all pursuit.
Without the Self, never could life exist.

The Self seems to move, but is ever still.
He seems far away, but is ever near.
He is within all, and he transcends all.

Those who see all creatures in themselves
And themselves in all creatures know no fear.
Those who see all creatures in themselves
And themselves in all creatures know no grief.
How can the multiplicity of life
Delude the one who sees its unity?

The Self is everywhere. Bright is the Self,
Indivisible, untouched by sin, wise,
Immanent and transcendent. He it is
Who holds the cosmos together.

In dark night live those for whom
The world without alone is real; in night
Darker still, for whom the world within
Alone is real. The first leads to a life
Of action, the second to a life of meditation.
But those who combine action with meditation
Cross the sea of death through action
And enter into immortality
Through the practice of meditation.
So have we heard from the wise.

In dark night live those for whom the Lord
Is transcendent only; in night darker still,
For whom he is immanent only.
But those for whom he is transcendent
And immanent cross the sea of death
With the immanent and enter into
Immortality with the transcendent.
So have we heard from the wise.
The face of truth is hidden by your orb
Of gold, O sun. May you remove your orb
So that I, who adore the true, may see
The glory of truth. O nourishing sun,
Solitary traveler, controller,
Source of life for all creatures, spread your light

And subdue your dazzling splendor
So that I may see your blessed Self.
Even that very Self am I!

OM shanti shanti shanti

—*From the Isha Upanishad*

You Are That

"THERE IS NOTHING that does not come from him.
Of everything he is the inmost Self.
He is the truth; he is the Self supreme.
You are that, Shvetaketu; you are that."

"Please, Father, tell me more about this Self."

"Yes, dear one, I will," Uddalaka said.
"Strike at the root of a tree; it would bleed
But still live. Strike again at the top;
It would bleed but still live. The Self as life
Supports the tree, which stands firm and enjoys
The nourishment it receives.
If the Self leaves one branch, that branch withers.
If it leaves a second, that too withers.
If it leaves a third, that again withers.
Let it leave the whole tree, the whole tree dies.
Just so, dear one, when death comes and the Self
Departs from the body, the body dies.
But the Self dies not.

"'There is nothing that does not come from him.
Of everything he is the inmost Self.
He is the truth; he is the Self supreme.
You are that, Shvetaketu; you are that."

"Please, Father, tell me more about this Self."
"Yes, dear one, I will," Uddalaka said.
"Bring me a fruit from the nyagrodha tree."

"Here it is, Sir."

"Break it. What do you see?"

"Nothing at all."

"That hidden essence you do not see, dear one,
From that a whole nyagrodha tree will grow.
There is nothing that does not come from him.
Of everything he is the inmost Self.
He is the truth; he is the Self supreme.
You are that, Shvetaketu; you are that."

"Please, Father, tell me more about this Self."

"Yes, dear one, I will," Uddalaka said.
"Place this salt in water and bring it here
Tomorrow morning." The boy did.
"Where is that salt?" his father asked.

"I do not see it."

"Sip here. How does it taste?"

"Salty, Father."

"And here? And there?"

"I taste salt everywhere."

"It *is* everywhere, though we see it not.
Just so, dear one, the Self is everywhere,

Within all things, although we see him not.
There is nothing that does not come from him.
Of everything he is the inmost Self.
He is the truth; he is the Self supreme.
You are that, Shvetaketu; you are that."

"Please, Father, tell me more about this Self."

"Yes, dear one, I will," Uddalaka said.

"As a man from Gandhara, blindfolded,
Led away and left in a lonely place,
Turns to the east and west and north and south
And shouts, 'I am left here and cannot see!'
Until one removes his blindfold and says,
'There lies Gandhara; follow that path,'
And thus informed, able to see for himself,
The man inquires from village to village
And reaches his homeland at last—just so,
My son, one who finds an illumined teacher
Attains to spiritual wisdom in the Self.
There is nothing that does not come from him.
Of everything he is the inmost Self.
He is the truth; he is the Self supreme.
You are that, Shvetaketu; you are that."

—*From the Chandogya Upanishad*

The Highest Mystical Teaching

ALL IS CHANGE in the world of the senses,
But changeless is the supreme Lord of Love.
Meditate on him, be absorbed in him,
Wake up from this dream of separateness.

Know God and all fetters will fall away.
No longer identifying yourself
With the body, go beyond birth and death.
All your desires will be fulfilled in him
Who is One without a second.

Know him to be enshrined in your heart always.
Truly there is nothing more in life to know.
Meditate and realize this world
Is filled with the presence of God.

Fire is not seen until one firestick rubs
Against another, though fire is still there,
Hidden in the firestick. So does the Lord
Remain hidden in the body until
He is revealed through the mystic mantram.

Let your body be the lower firestick;
Let the mantram be the upper. Rub them
Against each other in meditation
And realize the Lord.

Like oil in sesame seeds, like butter
In cream, like water in springs, like fire
In firesticks, so dwells the Lord of Love,
The Self, in the very depths of consciousness.
Realize him through truth and meditation.

The Self is hidden in the hearts of all,
As butter lies hidden in cream. Realize
The Self in the depths of meditation—
The Lord of Love, supreme Reality,
Who is the goal of all knowledge.

This is the highest mystical teaching;
This is the highest mystical teaching.

—*From the Shvetashvatara Upanishad*

The Sun That Dispels Our Darkness

I HAVE REALIZED the Lord of Love,
Who is the sun that dispels our darkness.
Those who realize him go beyond death;
No other way is there to immortality.

There is nothing higher than him, nothing other
Than him. His infinity is beyond great
And small. In his own glory rooted,
He stands and fills the cosmos.

He fills the cosmos, yet he transcends it.
Those who know him leave all separateness,
Sorrow, and death behind. Those who know him not
Live but suffer.

The Lord of Love, omnipresent, dwelling
In the heart of every living creature,
All mercy, turns every face to himself.

He is the supreme Lord, who through his grace
Moves us to seek him in our own hearts.
He is the light that shines forever.

He is the inner Self of all,
Hidden like a little flame in the heart.
Only by the stilled mind can he be known.
Those who realize him become immortal.

—From the Shvetashvatara Upanishad

His Face Is Everywhere

May the Lord of Love, who projects himself
Into this universe of myriad forms,
From whom all beings come and to whom all
Return, grant us the grace of wisdom.

He is fire and the sun, and the moon
And the stars. He is the air and the sea,
And the Creator, Prajapati.
He is this boy, he is that girl, he is
This man, he is that woman, and he is
This old man, too, tottering on his staff.
His face is everywhere.

He is the blue bird, he is the green bird
With red eyes; he is the thundercloud,
And he is the seasons and the seas.
He has no beginning, he has no end.
He is the source from which the worlds evolve.

From his divine power comes forth all this
Magical show of name and form, of you
And me, which casts the spell of pain and pleasure.
Only when we pierce through this magic veil
Do we see the One who appears as many.

Two birds of beautiful plumage, comrades
Inseparable, live on the selfsame tree.

One bird eats the fruit of pleasure and pain;
The other looks on without eating.

Forgetting our divine origin,
We become ensnared in the world of change
And bewail our helplessness. But when
We see the Lord of Love in all his glory,
Adored by all, we go beyond sorrow.

What use are the scriptures to anyone
Who knows not the one source from whom they come,
In whom all gods and worlds abide?
Only those who realize him as ever present
Within the heart attain abiding joy.

—*From the Shvetashvatara Upanishad*

Hear, O Children of Immortal Bliss

May we harness body and mind to see
The Lord of Life, who dwells in everyone.
May we ever with one-pointed mind
Strive for blissful union with the Lord.
May we train our senses to serve the Lord
Through the practice of meditation.

Great is the glory of the Lord of Life,
Infinite, omnipresent, all-knowing.
He is known by the wise who meditate
And conserve their vital energy.

Hear, O children of immortal bliss,
You are born to be united with the Lord.
Follow the path of the illumined ones
And be united with the Lord of Life.

Kindle the fire of kundalini deep
In meditation. Bring your mind and breath
Under control. Drink deep of divine love,
And you will attain the unitive state.

Dedicate yourself to the Lord of Life,
Who is the cause of the cosmos. He will
Remove the cause of all your suffering
And free you from the bondage of karma.

Be seated with spinal column erect
And turn your senses and mind deep within.
With the mantram echoing in your heart,
Cross over the dread sea of birth and death.

Train your senses to be obedient.
Regulate your activities to lead you
To the goal. Hold the reins of your mind
As you hold the reins of restive horses.

In deep meditation aspirants may
See forms like snow or smoke. They may feel
A strong wind blowing or a wave of heat.
They may see within them more and more light:
Fireflies, lightning, sun, or moon. These are signs
That one is far on the path to Brahman.

Health, a light body, freedom from cravings,
A glowing skin, sonorous voice, fragrance
Of body: these signs indicate progress
In the practice of meditation.

Those who attain the supreme goal of life,
Realizing the Self and passing beyond
All sorrow, shine bright as a mirror
Which has been cleansed of dust.

In the supreme climax of samadhi
They realize the presence of the Lord
Within their heart. Freed from impurities,
They pass forever beyond birth and death.

—*From the Shvetashvatara Upanishad*

In Praise of the Wise

THE WISE have attained the unitive state,
And see only the resplendent Lord of Love.
Desiring nothing in the physical world,
They have become one with the Lord of Love.

Those who dwell on and long for sense-pleasure
Are born in a world of separateness.
But let them realize they are the Self
And all separateness will fall away.

Not through discourse, not through the intellect,
Not even through study of the scriptures
Can the Self be realized. The Self reveals
Himself to the one who longs for the Self.
Those who long for the Self with all their heart
Are chosen by the Self as his own.

Not by the weak, not by the unearnest,
Not by those who practice wrong disciplines
Can the Self be realized. The Self reveals
Himself as the Lord of Love to the one
Who practices right disciplines.

What the sages sought they have found at last.
No more questions have they to ask of life.
With self-will extinguished, they are at peace.
Seeing the Lord of Love in all around,

Serving the Lord of Love in all around,
They are united with him forever.

They have attained the summit of wisdom
By the steep path of renunciation.
They have attained to immortality
And are united with the Lord of Love.
When they leave the body, the vital force
Returns to the cosmic womb, but their work
Becomes a beneficial force in life
To bring others together in the Self.

—From the Mundaka Upanishad

The Unitive State

THE SELF, pure awareness, shines as the light within the heart, surrounded by the senses. Only seeming to think, seeming to move, the Self neither sleeps nor wakes nor dreams.

When the Self takes on a body, he seems to assume the body's frailties and limitations; but when he sheds the body at the time of death, the Self leaves all these behind.

The human being has two states of consciousness: one in this world, the other in the next. But there is a third state between them, not unlike the world of dreams, in which we are aware of both worlds, with their sorrows and joys. When a person dies, it is only the physical body that dies; that person lives on in a nonphysical body, which carries the impressions of his past life. It is these impressions that determine his next life. In this intermediate state he makes and dissolves impressions by the light of the Self.

In that third state of consciousness there are no chariots, no horses drawing them or roads on which to travel, but he makes up his own chariots, horses, and roads. In that state there are no joys or pleasures, but he makes up his own joys and pleasures. In that state there are no lotus ponds, no lakes, no rivers, but he makes up his own lotus ponds, lakes, and rivers. It is he who makes up all these from the impressions of his past or waking life.

It is said of these states of consciousness that in the dreaming state, when one is sleeping, the shining Self, who never dreams, who is ever awake, watches by his own light the dreams woven out of past deeds and present desires. In the dreaming state, when one is sleeping, the shining Self keeps the body alive with the vital force of prana, and wanders wherever he wills. In the dreaming state, when one is sleeping, the shining Self assumes many forms, eats with friends, indulges in sex, sees fearsome spectacles. But he is not affected by anything because he is detached and free; and after wandering here and there in the state of dreaming, enjoying pleasures and seeing good and evil, he returns to the state from which he began.

As a great fish swims between the banks of a river as it likes, so does the shining Self move between the states of dreaming and waking.

As a man in the arms of his beloved is not aware of what is without and what is within, so a person in union with the Self is not aware of what is without and what is within, for in that unitive state all desires find their perfect fulfillment. There is no other desire that needs to be fulfilled, and one goes beyond sorrow.

In that unitive state there is neither father nor mother, neither worlds nor gods nor even scriptures. In that state there is neither thief nor slayer, neither low caste nor high, neither monk nor ascetic. The Self is beyond good and evil, beyond all the suffering of the human heart.

In that unitive state one sees without seeing, for there is nothing separate from him; smells without smelling, for there is nothing separate from him; tastes without tasting, for there is nothing separate from him; speaks without speaking, for there is nothing separate from him; hears without hearing, for there is nothing separate from him; touches without touching, for there is nothing separate from him; thinks without thinking, for there is nothing separate from him; knows without knowing, for there is nothing separate from him.

Where there is separateness, one sees another, smells another, tastes another, speaks to another, hears another, touches another, thinks of another, knows another. But where there is unity, one without a second, that is the world of Brahman. This is the supreme goal of life, the supreme treasure, the supreme joy. Those who do not seek this supreme goal live on but a fraction of this joy.

—*From the Brihadaranyaka Upanishad*

On the Greatness of "AUM"

AUM STANDS for the supreme Reality.
It is a symbol for what was, what is,
And what shall be. AUM represents also
What lies beyond past, present, and future.

Brahman is all, and the Self is Brahman.
This Self has four states of consciousness.

The first is called Vaishvanara, in which
One lives with all the senses turned outward,
Aware only of the external world.

Taijasa is the name of the second,
The dreaming state in which, with the senses
Turned inward, one enacts the impressions
Of past deeds and present desires.

The third state is called Prajna, of deep sleep,
In which one neither dreams nor desires.
There is no mind in Prajna, there is no
Separateness; but the sleeper is not
Conscious of this. Let him become conscious
In Prajna and it will open the door
To the state of abiding joy.

Prajna, all-powerful and all-knowing,
Dwells in the hearts of all as the ruler.
Prajna is the source and end of all.

The fourth is the superconscious state called
Turiya, neither inward nor outward,
Beyond the senses and the intellect,
In which there is none other than the Lord.
He is the supreme goal of life. He is
Infinite peace and love. Realize him!

Turiya is represented by AUM.
Though indivisible, it has three sounds.

A stands for Vaishvanara. Those who know this,
Through mastery of the senses, obtain
The fruit of their desires and attain greatness.

U indicates Taijasa. Those who know this,
By mastering even their dreams, become
Established in wisdom. In their family
Everyone leads the spiritual life.

M corresponds to Prajna. Those who know this,
By stilling the mind, find their true stature
And inspire everyone around to grow.

The mantram AUM stands for the supreme state
Of Turiya, without parts, beyond birth
And death, symbol of everlasting joy.
Those who know AUM as the Self become the Self;
Truly they become the Self.

OM shanti shanti shanti

—From the Mandukya Upanishad

To the Householder

Practice right conduct, learning and teaching;
Be truthful always, learning and teaching;
Master the passions, learning and teaching;
Control the senses, learning and teaching;
Strive for peace always, learning and teaching;
Rouse kundalini, learning and teaching;
Serve humanity, learning and teaching;
Beget progeny, learning and teaching.
Satyavacha says: "Be truthful always."
Taponitya says: "Master the passions."
Naka declares: "Learning and teaching are
Necessary for spiritual progress."

—From the Taittiriya Upanishad

What the Thunder Said

THE CHILDREN of Prajapati, the Creator—gods, human beings, and asuras, the godless—lived with their father as students. When they had completed the allotted period the gods said, "Venerable One, please teach us." Prajapati answered with one syllable: "*Da.*"

"Have you understood?" he asked.

"Yes," they said. "You have told us *damyata*, be self-controlled."

"You have understood," he said.

The human beings approached. "Venerable One, please teach us."

Prajapati answered with one syllable: "*Da.*"

"Have you understood?" he asked.

"Yes," they said. "You have told us *datta*, give."

"You have understood," he said.

Then the godless approached. "Venerable One, please teach us."

Prajapati answered with the same syllable: "*Da.*"

"Have you understood?" he asked.

"Yes," they said. "You have told us *dayadhvam*, be compassionate."

"You have understood," he said.

The heavenly voice of the thunder repeats this teaching. *Da-da-da!* Be self-controlled! Give! Be compassionate!

OM shanti shanti shanti

—*From the Brihadaranyaka Upanishad*

For the Love of the Soul

"Maitreyi," said one day Yajnavalkya to his wife, "I am going to leave this present life, and retire to a life of meditation. Let me settle my possessions upon you and Katyayani."

"If all the earth filled with riches belonged to me, O my Lord," said Maitreyi, "should I thereby attain life eternal?"

"Certainly not," said Yajnavalkya, "your life would only be as is the life of wealthy people. In wealth there is no hope of life eternal."

Maitreyi said: "What should I then do with possessions that cannot give me life eternal? Give me instead your knowledge, O my Lord."

On hearing this Yajnavalkya exclaimed: "Dear you are to me, beloved, and dear are the words you say. Come, sit down and I will teach; but hear my words with deep attention."

Then spoke Yajnavalkya:

"In truth, it is not for the love of a husband that a husband is dear; but for the love of the Soul in the husband that a husband is dear.

"It is not for the love of a wife that a wife is dear; but for the love of the Soul in the wife that a wife is dear.

"It is not for the love of children that children are dear; but for the love of the Soul in children that children are dear.

"It is not for the love of riches that riches are dear; but for the love of the Soul in riches that riches are dear.

"It is not for the love of religion that religion is dear; but for the love of the Soul in religion that religion is dear.

"It is not for the love of power that power is dear; but for the love of the Soul in power that power is dear.

"It is not for the love of the heavens that the heavens are dear; but for the love of the Soul in the heavens that the heavens are dear.

"It is not for the love of the gods that the gods are dear; but for the love of the Soul in the gods that the gods are dear.

"It is not for the love of creatures that creatures are dear; but for the love of the Soul in creatures that creatures are dear.

"It is not for the love of the all that the all is dear; but for the love of the Soul in the all that the all is dear.

"It is the Soul, the Spirit, the Self, that must be seen and be heard and have our thoughts and meditation, O Maitreyi. When the Soul is seen and heard, is thought upon and is known, then all that is becomes known.

"Religion will abandon the man who thinks that religion is apart from the Soul.

"Power will abandon the man who thinks that power is apart from the Soul.

"The gods will abandon the man who thinks that the gods are apart from the Soul.

"Creatures will abandon the man who thinks that creatures are apart from the Soul.

"And all will abandon the man who thinks that the all is apart from the Soul. Because religion, power, heavens, beings, gods and all rest on the Soul."

—*From the Brihadaranyaka Upanishad*

How to Work

SRI KRISHNA: You have the right to work, but never to the fruit of work. You should never engage in action for the sake of reward, nor should you long for inaction. Perform work in this world, Arjuna, as a man established within himself—without selfish attachments, and alike in success and defeat. For yoga is perfect evenness of mind.

Seek refuge in the attitude of detachment and you will amass the wealth of spiritual awareness. Those who are motivated only by desire for the fruits of action are miserable, for they are constantly anxious about the results of what they do. When consciousness is unified, however, all vain anxiety is left behind. There is no cause for worry, whether things go well or ill. Therefore, devote yourself to the disciplines of yoga, for yoga is skill in action.

The wise unify their consciousness and abandon attachment to the fruits of action, which binds a person to continual rebirth. Thus they attain a state beyond all evil.

When your mind has overcome the confusion of duality, you will attain the state of holy indifference to things you hear and things you have heard. When you are unmoved by the confusion of ideas and your mind is completely united in deep samadhi, you will attain the state of perfect yoga.

—From the Bhagavad Gita

What Is Action and What Is Inaction?

SRI KRISHNA: Actions do not cling to me because I am not attached to their results. Those who understand this and practice it live in freedom. Knowing this truth, aspirants desiring liberation in ancient times engaged in action. You too can do the same, pursuing an active life in the manner of those ancient sages.

What is action and what is inaction? This question has confused the greatest sages. I will give you the secret of action, with which you can free yourself from bondage. The true nature of action is difficult to grasp. You must understand what is action and what is inaction, and what kind of action should be avoided.

The wise see that there is action in the midst of inaction and inaction in the midst of action. Their consciousness is unified, and every act is done with complete awareness.

The awakened sages call a person wise when all his undertakings are free from anxiety about results; all his selfish desires have been consumed in the fire of knowledge. The wise, ever satisfied, have abandoned all external supports. Their security is unaffected by the results of their action; even while acting, they really do nothing at all. Free from expectations and from all sense of possession, with mind and body firmly controlled by the Self, they do not incur sin by the performance of physical action.

They live in freedom who have gone beyond the dualities of life. Competing with no one, they are alike in success and failure and content with whatever comes to them. They are free, without selfish attachments; their minds are fixed in knowledge. They perform all work in the spirit of service, and their karma is dissolved.

The process of offering is Brahman; that which is offered is Brahman. Brahman offers the sacrifice in the fire of Brahman. Brahman is attained by those who see Brahman in every action.

Some aspirants offer material sacrifices to the gods. Others offer selfless service as sacrifice in the fire of Brahman. Some renounce all enjoyment of the senses, sacrificing them in the fire of sense restraint. Others partake of sense objects but offer them in service through the fire of the senses. Some offer the workings of the senses and the vital forces through the fire of self-control, kindled in the path of knowledge.

Some offer wealth; others offer sense restraint and suffering. Some take vows and offer knowledge and study of the scriptures; and some make the offering of meditation. Some offer the forces of vitality, regulating their inhalation and exhalation, and thus gain control over these forces. Others offer the forces of vitality through restraint of their senses. All these understand the meaning of service and will be cleansed of their impurities.

True sustenance is in service, and through it a man or woman reaches the eternal Brahman. But those who do not seek to serve are without a home in this world. Arjuna, how can they be at home in any world to come?

These offerings are born of work, and each guides mankind along a path to Brahman.

—*From the Bhagavad Gita*

The Royal Path of Devotion

SRI KRISHNA: Whatever I am offered in devotion with a pure heart—a leaf, a flower, fruit, or water—I partake of that love offering. Whatever you do, make it an offering to me—the food you eat, the sacrifices you make, the help you give, even your suffering. In this way you will be freed from the bondage of karma, and from its results both pleasant and painful. Then, firm in renunciation and yoga, with your heart free, you will come to me.

I look upon all creatures equally; none are less dear to me and none more dear. But those who worship me with love live in me, and I come to life in them.

Even a sinner becomes holy when he worships me alone with firm resolve. Quickly his soul conforms to dharma and he attains to boundless peace. Never forget this, Arjuna: no one who is devoted to me will ever come to harm.

All those who take refuge in me, whatever their birth, race, sex, or caste, will attain the supreme goal; this realization can be attained even by those whom society scorns. Kings and sages too seek this goal with devotion. Therefore, having been born in this transient and forlorn world, give all your love to me. Fill your mind with me; love me; serve me; worship me always. Seeking me in your heart, you will at last be united with me.

—From the Bhagavad Gita

The Cosmic Vision

ARJUNA: Out of compassion you have taught me the supreme mystery of the Self. Through your words my delusion is gone. You have explained the origin and end of every creature, O lotus-eyed one, and told me of your own supreme, limitless existence.

Just as you have described your infinite glory, O Lord, now I long to see it. I want to see you as the supreme ruler of creation. O Lord, master of yoga, if you think me strong enough to behold it, show me your immortal Self.

SRI KRISHNA: Behold, Arjuna, a million divine forms, with an infinite variety of color and shape. Behold the gods of the natural world, and many more wonders never revealed before. Behold the entire cosmos turning within my body, and the other things you desire to see.

But these things cannot be seen with your physical eyes; therefore I give you spiritual vision to perceive my majestic power.

SANJAYA: Having spoken these words, Krishna, the master of yoga, revealed to Arjuna his most exalted, lordly form.

He appeared with an infinite number of faces, ornamented by heavenly jewels, displaying unending miracles and the countless weapons of his power. Clothed in celestial garments and covered with garlands, sweet-smelling with heavenly fragrances, he showed himself as the infinite Lord, the source of all wonders, whose face is everywhere.

If a thousand suns were to rise in the heavens at the

same time, the blaze of their light would resemble the splendor of that supreme spirit.

There, within the body of the god of gods, Arjuna saw all the manifold forms of the universe united as one. Filled with amazement, his hair standing on end in ecstasy, he bowed before the Lord with joined palms and spoke these words.

ARJUNA: O Lord, I see within your body all the gods and every kind of living creature. I see Brahma, the Creator, seated on a lotus; I see the ancient sages and the celestial serpents.

I see infinite mouths and arms, stomachs and eyes, and you are embodied in every form. I see you everywhere, without beginning, middle, or end. You are the Lord of all creation, and the cosmos is your body.

You wear a crown and carry a mace and discus; your radiance is blinding and immeasurable. I see you, who are so difficult to behold, shining like a fiery sun blazing in every direction. You are the supreme, changeless Reality, the one thing to be known. You are the refuge of all creation, the immortal spirit, the eternal guardian of eternal dharma.

You are without beginning, middle, or end; you touch everything with your infinite power. The sun and moon are your eyes, and your mouth is fire; your radiance warms the cosmos.

O Lord, your presence fills the heavens and the earth and reaches in every direction. I see the three worlds trembling before this vision of your wonderful and terrible form.

The gods enter your being, some calling out and greeting you in fear. Great saints sing your glory, praying, "May all be well!"

The multitudes of gods, demigods, and demons are all overwhelmed by the sight of you. O mighty Lord, at the sight of your myriad eyes and mouths, arms and legs, stomachs and fearful teeth, I and the entire universe shake in terror.

O Vishnu, I can see your eyes shining; with open mouth, you glitter in an array of colors, and your body touches the sky. I look at you and my heart trembles; I have lost all courage and all peace of mind.

When I see your mouths with their fearful teeth, mouth burning like the fires at the end of time, I forget where I am and I have no place to go. O Lord, you are the support of the universe; have mercy on me!

You lap the worlds into your burning mouths and swallow them. Filled with your terrible radiance, O Vishnu, the whole of creation bursts into flames.

—From the Bhagavad Gita

The Way of Love

ARJUNA: Of those steadfast devotees who love you and those who seek you as the eternal formless Reality, who are the more established in yoga?

SRI KRISHNA: Those who set their hearts on me and worship me with unfailing devotion and faith are more established in yoga.

As for those who seek the transcendental Reality, without name, without form, contemplating the Unmanifested, beyond the reach of thought and of feeling, with their senses subdued and mind serene and striving for the good of all beings, they too will verily come unto me.

Yet hazardous and slow is the path to the Unrevealed, difficult for physical man to tread. But they for whom I am the supreme goal, who do all work renouncing self for me and meditate on me with single-hearted devotion, these I will swiftly rescue from the fragment's cycle of birth and death, for their consciousness has entered into me.

Still your mind in me, still your intellect in me, and without doubt you will be united with me forever. If you cannot still your mind in me, learn to do so through the regular practice of meditation. If you lack the will for such self-discipline, engage yourself in my work, for selfless service can lead you at last to complete fulfillment. If you are unable to do even this, surrender yourself to me, disciplining yourself and renouncing the results of all your actions.

Better indeed is knowledge than mechanical practice.

Better than knowledge is meditation. But better still is surrender of attachment to results, because there follows immediate peace.

That one I love who is incapable of ill will, who is friendly and compassionate. Living beyond the reach of *I* and *mine* and of pleasure and pain, patient, contented, self-controlled, firm in faith, with all his heart and all his mind given to me—with such a one I am in love.

Not agitating the world or by it agitated, he stands above the sway of elation, competition, and fear: he is my beloved.

—*From the Bhagavad Gita*

Devotion to Duty

SRI KRISHNA: By devotion to one's own particular duty, everyone can attain perfection. Let me tell you how. By performing his own work, one worships the Creator who dwells in every creature. Such worship brings that person to fulfillment.

It is better to perform one's own duties imperfectly than to master the duties of another. By fulfilling the obligations he is born with, a person never comes to grief. No one should abandon duties because he sees defects in them. Every action, every activity, is surrounded by defects as a fire is surrounded by smoke.

Make every act an offering to me; regard me as your only protector. Relying on interior discipline, meditate on me always. Remembering me, you shall overcome all difficulties through my grace. But if you will not heed me in your self-will, nothing will avail you.

If you egotistically say, "I will not fight this battle," your resolve will be useless; your own nature will drive you into it. Your own karma, born of your own nature, will drive you to do even that which you do not wish to do, because of your delusion.

The Lord dwells in the hearts of all creatures and whirls them round upon the wheel of maya. Run to him for refuge with all your strength, and peace profound will be yours through his grace.

Be aware of me always, adore me, make every act an offering to me, and you shall come to me; this I promise;

for you are dear to me. Abandon all supports and look to me for protection. I shall purify you from the sins of the past; do not grieve.

—*From the Bhagavad Gita*

The Goddess Reveals Her Cosmic Body

THE GODDESS SPOKE:

I imagine into being the whole world, moving and unmoving, through the power of my Maya,

Yet that same Maya is not separate from me; this is the highest truth . . .

In me this whole world is woven in all directions, O Mountain.

I am the Lord and the Cosmic Soul; I am myself the Cosmic Body.

I am Brahma, Vishnu, and Rudra, as well as Gauri, Brahmi, and Vaishnavi.

I am the sun and the stars and I am the Lord of the stars.

I am the various species of beasts and birds; I am also the outcaste and thief.

I am the evil doer and the wicked deed; I am the righteous person and the virtuous deed.

I am certainly female and male, and asexual as well.

And whatever thing, anywhere, you see or hear,

That entire thing I pervade, ever abiding inside it and outside.

There is nothing at all, moving or unmoving, that is devoid of me;

For if it were, it would be a nonentity, like the son of a barren woman.

Just as a single rope may appear variously as a serpent or wreath,

So also I may appear in the form of the Lord and the like; there is no doubt in this matter.

The world cannot appear without an underlying basis.
Accordingly, the world comes to be only through my own
being and in no other way.

—*From the Devi Gita*

The Goddess Explains at Length the Supreme Devotion Beyond the Gunas

Now be attentive while I explain the highest kind of
   devotion.
One who constantly listens to my virtues and recites my
   names,
Who is firmly intent on me, a treasury of auspicious
   qualities,
Whose concentration is ever steady like a continuous flow
   of oil,
Who has no ulterior motive at all in these actions,
Having no desire for liberation in any form—whether living
   in my presence, sharing my powers, merging into me, or
   dwelling in my heaven—
Who knows absolutely nothing better than serving me,
Cherishing the notion of servant and master and thus not
   aspiring even for liberation,
Who enthusiastically thinks of me alone with supreme
   affection,
Knowing me truly as never separate from oneself, not
   acknowledging any difference,
Who thinks of beings as embodiments of myself, loving
   other selves as one's own Self;
Who makes no false distinctions, realizing the universality
   of pure consciousness,
My omnipresent essence manifested in all beings
   everywhere at all times,

Who honors and respects even the lowest outcaste, O Lord,
Discarding any sense of difference and thus wishing harm
　　to no one,
Who is eager to see my sacred sites and to see my devotees,
And is eager to listen to scriptures that describe the
　　mantras and rites used in worshipping me, O Ruler,
Whose heart is overwhelmed with love for me, whose body
　　ever thrills with joy,
Whose eyes are filled with tears of love, and whose voice
　　falters,
Who, with such enraptured feelings, O Mountain Chief,
　　worships
Me as ruler, womb of the world, and cause of all causes,
Who performs my splendrous rites, both the regular and
　　the occasional, always with devotion and without miserly
　　regard for cost,
Who longs to see my festivals and to participate in them,
Ever impelled by such desires arising spontaneously, O
　　Mountain,
Who sings on high my names while dancing,
Unselfconscious and forgetful of the body,
Who accepts the fruits of past karma as what must be,
Unconcerned with thoughts of preserving the body,
Such a person practices devotion deemed supreme,
In which there is no thought of anything except me, the
　　Goddess.
The person in whom such supreme devotion truly arises, O
　　Mountain,
Then dissolves into my essential nature of pure
　　consciousness.

—From the Devi Gita

The Tantric Praise of the Goddess

WE bow to the Goddess, to the Great Goddess, to the Energy of Infinite Goodness at all times we bow. We bow to nature, to the Excellent One, with discipline we have bowed down.

To the Reliever of Sufferings we bow, to the Eternal, to the Embodiment of Rays of Light, to the Creatress, to She Who Manifests Light, to the form of Devotion, to Happiness continually we bow.

To the welfare of those who bow, we bow; to Change, to Perfection, to Dissolution, to the Wealth which sustains the earth, to the Wife of Consciousness, to you, we bow, we bow.

To She who Removes Difficulties, to She Who Removes Beyond All Difficulties, to the Essence, to the Cause of All; to Perception, and to the Doer of All, to the Unknowable One, continually we bow.

To the extremely beautiful and to the extremely fierce, we bow to Her, we bow, we bow. We bow to the Establisher of the Perceivable Universe, to the Goddess, to All Action, we bow, we bow.

To the Divine Goddess in all existence who is addressed as the Perceivable Form of the Consciousness Which

Pervades All, we bow to Her; we bow to Her; we bow to Her, continually we bow, we bow.

To the Divine Goddess in all existence who resides all throughout the Consciousness and is known by the reflections of mind, we bow to Her; we bow to Her; we bow to Her, continually we bow, we bow.

To the Divine Goddess who resides in all existence in the form of Intelligence, we bow to Her; we bow to Her; we bow to Her, continually we bow, we bow.

To the Divine Goddess who resides in all existence in the form of Sleep, we bow to Her; we bow to Her; we bow to Her, continually we bow, we bow.

To the Divine Goddess who resides in all existence in the form of Hunger, we bow to Her; we bow to Her; we bow to Her, continually we bow, we bow.

To the Divine Goddess who resides in all existence in the form of Appearance, we bow to Her; we bow to Her; we bow to Her, continually we bow, we bow.

To the Divine Goddess who resides in all existence in the form of Energy, we bow to Her; we bow to Her; we bow to Her, continually we bow, we bow.

To the Divine Goddess who resides in all existence in the form of Desire, we bow to Her; we bow to Her; we bow to Her, continually we bow, we bow.

To the Divine Goddess who resides in all existence in the form of Patient Forgiveness, we bow to Her; we bow to Her; we bow to Her, continually we bow, we bow.

To the Divine Goddess who resides in all existence in the form of All Living Beings, we bow to Her; we bow to Her; we bow to Her, continually we bow, we bow.

To the Divine Goddess who resides in all existence in the form of Humility, we bow to Her; we bow to Her; we bow to Her, continually we bow, we bow.

To the Divine Goddess who resides in all existence in the form of Peace, we bow to Her; we bow to Her; we bow to Her, continually we bow, we bow.

To the Divine Goddess who resides in all existence in the form of Faith, we bow to Her; we bow to Her; we bow to Her, continually we bow, we bow.

To the Divine Goddess who resides in all existence in the form of Beauty Enhanced by Love, we bow to Her; we bow to Her; we bow to Her, continually we bow, we bow.

To the Divine Goddess who resides in all existence in the form of True Wealth, we bow to Her; we bow to Her; we bow to Her, continually we bow, we bow.

To the Divine Goddess who resides in all existence in the form of Activity, we bow to Her; we bow to Her; we bow to Her, continually we bow, we bow.

To the Divine Goddess who resides in all existence in the form of Recollection, we bow to Her; we bow to Her; we bow to Her, continually we bow, we bow.

To the Divine Goddess who resides in all existence in the form of Compassion, we bow to Her; we bow to Her; we bow to Her, continually we bow, we bow.

To the Divine Goddess who resides in all existence in the form of Satisfaction, we bow to Her; we bow to Her; we bow to Her, continually we bow, we bow.

To the Divine Goddess who resides in all existence in the form of Mother, we bow to Her; we bow to Her; we bow to Her, continually we bow, we bow.

To the Divine Goddess who resides in all existence in the form of Confusion, we bow to Her; we bow to Her; we bow to Her, continually we bow, we bow.

Presiding over the senses of all beings and pervading all existence, to the Omnipresent Goddess who individualizes creation we bow, we bow.

In the form of Consciousness She distinguishes the individual phenomena of the perceivable universe. We bow to Her; we bow to Her; we bow to Her, continually we bow, we bow.

In days of old, all of the Gods, led by Indra, the Rule of the Pure, sang these verses of praise for the purpose of accomplishing their desired objective of surrendering the ego in the Light of Wisdom, and for many days that service was rendered. May She, the Seer of All, the Lord of All, the Source of All Good, perform similarly for us all auspicious things by putting an end to all distress.

We Gods have been harassed by arrogant thoughts in the manner of men, and at this time all of us Gods bow to the Seer of All, who, when bowed to with devotion, and remembered in a physical image, immediately terminates our every adversity.

—From the Chandi Patha

The Six Stanzas of Salvation

I AM neither the mind, the intellect, nor the silent voice
    within;
Neither the eyes, the ears, the nose, nor the mouth.
I am not water, fire, earth, nor ether—
I am Consciousness and Bliss.
        I am Shiva! I am Shiva!

I am not the life-force nor the vital airs;
Not the seven components nor the five sheaths.
I am not the tongue, hands, feet, nor organ of procreation—
I am Consciousness and Bliss.
        I am Shiva! I am Shiva!

Neither attachment nor aversion can touch me;
Neither greed, delusion, pride, nor jealousy are mine at all.
I am not duty, nor wealth, nor happiness—
I am Consciousness and Bliss.
        I am Shiva! I am Shiva!

I am not virtue nor vice; not pain nor pleasure;
I am neither temple nor holy word; not sacred fire nor the
    Vedas—
I am Consciousness and Bliss.
        I am Shiva! I am Shiva!

I have neither death, nor doubt, nor class distinction;
Neither father nor mother, nor any birth at all.

I am not the brother, the friend, the Master, nor the
   disciple—
I am Consciousness and Bliss.
     I am Shiva! I am Shiva!

I am not detachment nor salvation,
nor anything reached by the senses;
I am beyond all thought and form.
I am everywhere, and nowhere at all—
I am Consciousness and Bliss.
     I am Shiva! I am Shiva!

                  —*Shankaracharya*

In the Fire of Knowledge

JUST AS a stone, a tree, a straw, grain, a mat, a cloth, a pot, and so on, when burned, are reduced to earth (from which they came), so the body and its sense organs, on being burned in the fire of Knowledge, become Knowledge and are absorbed in Brahman, like darkness in the light of the sun. When a pot is broken the space that was in it becomes one with space; so too when the limitation caused by the body and its adjuncts is removed the Sage, realized during life, shines as Brahman, becoming absorbed in Brahman he already was, like milk in milk, water in water, or oil in oil, and is radiant as the One Supreme Self.

Thus, when the Sage who abides as Brahman, which is Pure Being, obtains his disembodied absolute state, he is never again reborn. How can there be rebirth for a Sage who abides as Brahman, his body and its limitations burned by the fire of Knowledge, the Identity of individual and Supreme? The existence of all that is either affirmed or denied in the one substratum of the indestructible, unattached, nondual, absolute Self depends only on the mind, just as the appearance or disappearance of the imaginary snake in a piece of rope has no basis in reality. Bondage and Liberation are creations of Maya, superimpositions upon the Brahman imagined by the mind without any existence in reality. It is a fool who blames the sun for his own blindness. . . . The scriptures even proclaim aloud: "There is in truth no creation and no destruction; no one is bound, no one is seeking Liberation, no one is on the way to Deliverance. There are none Liberated. This is the absolute truth." My dear disciple, this, the sum and substance of all the Upanishads, the secret of secrets, is my instruction to you.

—*Shankaracharya*

Awareness: I Am the Infinite Ocean

YESTERDAY
I lived bewildered,
In illusion.

But now I am awake,
Flawless and serene,
Beyond the world.

From my light
The body and the world arise.

So all things are mine,
Or nothing is.

Now I have given up
The body and the world,
I have a special gift.

I see the infinite Self.

As a wave,
Seething and foaming,
Is only water

So all creation,
Streaming out of the Self,
Is only the Self.

Consider a piece of cloth.
It is only threads!

So all creation,
When you look closely,
Is only the Self.

Like the sugar
In the juice of the sugarcane,
I am the sweetness
In everything I have made.

When the Self is unknown
The world arises,
Not when it is known.

But you mistake
The rope for the snake.

When you see the rope,
The snake vanishes.

My nature is light,
Nothing but light.

When the world arises
I alone am shining.

When the world arises in me,
It is just an illusion:
Water shimmering in the sun,

A vein of silver in mother-of-pearl,
A serpent in a strand of rope.

From me the world streams out
And in me it dissolves,
As a bracelet melts into gold,
A pot crumbles into clay,
A wave subsides into water.

I adore myself.
How wonderful I am!

I can never die.

The whole world may perish,
From Brahma to a blade of grass,
But I am still here.

Indeed how wonderful!
I adore myself.

For I have taken form
But I am still one.

Neither coming or going,
Yet I am still everywhere. . . .

I am the infinite ocean.

When thoughts spring up,
The wind freshens, and like waves
A thousand worlds arise.

But when the wind falls,
The trader sinks with his ship.

On the boundless ocean of my being
He founders,
And all the worlds with him.

But O how wonderful!

I am the unbounded deep
In whom all living things
Naturally arise,
Rush against each other playfully,
And then subside.

—*From the Ashtavakra Gita*

The Story of the Rock

THERE IS a great rock which is full of tenderness and affection, which is obvious and ever clearly perceived, which is soft, which is omnipresent and eternal. Within it countless lotuses blossom. Their petals sometimes touch one another, sometimes not; sometimes they are exposed and sometimes they are hidden from view. Some face downward, some face upward and some have their roots intertwined. Some have no roots at all. All things exist within it, though they do not.

O Rama, this rock is indeed the cosmic consciousness; it is rocklike in its homogeneity. Yet within it all diverse creatures of this universe appear to be. Just as one conceives or imagines different forms within the rock, the universe is also ignorantly imagined to exist in this consciousness. Even if a sculptor "creates" different forms in the rock, it is still rock: even so in the case of this cosmic consciousness that is a homogeneous mass of consciousness. Even as the solid rock contains potentially diverse figures which can be carved out of it, the diverse names and forms of the creatures of this universe exist potentially in cosmic consciousness. Even as rock remains rock, carved or uncarved, consciousness remains consciousness whether the world appears or not. The world-appearance is but an empty expression; its substance is nothing but consciousness.

In fact, even these manifestations and modifications are but Brahman, the cosmic consciousness—though not in the sense of manifestation or modification. Even this distinction—modification in the sense of modification, or any other sense—is meaningless in Brahman. When such expressions are used in relation to Brahman, the meaning is quite different, like water in the mirage. Since the seed does not contain anything other than the seed, even the flowers and the fruits are of the same nature as the seed: the substance of the seed is the substance of subsequent effects, too. Even so, the homogeneous mass of cosmic consciousness does not give rise to anything other than what it is in essence. When this truth is realized, duality ceases.

—*From the Yoga Vasishtha*

The Nectar of Self-Awareness

I HONOR the God and the Goddess,
The eternal parents of the universe.

The Lover, out of boundless love,
 takes the form of the Beloved.
What Beauty!
Both are made of the same nectar
 and share the same food.

Out of Supreme love
 they swallow up each other
But separate again
 for the joy of being two.

They are not completely the same
 but neither are they different.
No one can tell exactly what they are.

How intense is their longing
 to be with each other.
This is their greatest bliss.
Never, not even in jest,
Do they allow their unity
 to be disturbed.

They are so averse to separation
That even though they have become
 this entire world,

Never for a moment do they let a difference
        come between them.

Even though they see
        all that is animate and inanimate,
        arising from within themselves,
They never recognize a third.

They sit together
        in the same place,
Both wearing a garment of light.
From the beginning of time
        they have been together,
Reveling in their own Supreme Love.

They created a difference
        to enjoy this world.
When that "difference" had one glimpse of their intimacy
It could not help
        but merge back into the bliss
        of their eternal union.

Without the God,
        there is no Goddess,
And without the Goddess,
        there is no God.

How sweet is their love!
The entire universe
        is too small to contain them,

Yet they live happily
        in the tiniest particle.

The life of one
        is the life of the other,
And not even a blade of grass can grow
        without both of them.

Only these two live
        in this house called the universe.
When either one is asleep
The other stays awake
        and plays the part of both.

Should both of them awake,
The whole universe would vanish
        without a trace.

They become two
        for the sake of divine play,
But in every moment
        they seek to become one again. . . .

How can we distinguish these two from each other?
He appears because of Her,
And She exists because of Him.

We cannot tell sugar
        from its sweetness,
Nor camphor
        from its fragrance.

To capture light
  we take hold of fire.
To capture the Supreme Shiva
  we must take hold of Shakti.

Light illumines the Sun,
But the Sun itself
  creates that light.
The glorious Sun and its light
  are one and the same.

An object has a reflection:
When looking we see two images,
  yet there is only one thing.
Likewise, this world is a reflection
  of the Supreme Lord.

We may see two,
Yet only One exists. . . .

Shiva and Shakti are one,
Like air and the wind,
Like gold and its luster.

Shiva and Shakti cannot be separated
They are like musk and its fragrance,
  like fire and its heat.

In the light of the Sun
  there is no difference between day and night.

In the light of the Supreme Truth
    there is no difference between Shiva and Shakti.

Shiva and Shakti envy the Primordial Sound "OM"
    because they are seen as two
    while the sound OM is always regarded as one.

Jnanadeva says,
"I honor the union of Shiva and Shakti,
    who devour this world of name and form
    like a sweet dish.
All that remains is the One."

—*Jnaneshwar (also known as Jnanadeva)*

This Miracle

I'M THE ONE who has the body,
you're the one who holds the breath.

You know the secret of my body,
I know the secret of your breath.

That's why your body
is in mine.

You know
and I know, Ramanatha,

the miracle

of your breath
in my body.

—*Devara Dasimayya*

Show Me Your Way Out

LIKE A SILKWORM weaving
her house with love
from her marrow,
        and dying
in her body's threads
winding tight, round
and round,
        I burn
desiring what the heart desires.

Cut through, O lord,
my heart's greed,
and show me
your way out,

O lord white as jasmine.

—*Mahadeviyakka*

O Lord White As Jasmine

You're like milk
in water: I cannot tell
what comes before,
what after;
which is the master,
which is the slave;
what's big,
what's small.

O lord white as jasmine
if an ant should love you
and praise you,
will he not grow
to demon powers?

—*Mahadeviyakka*

If My Head Falls from My Shoulders

IF SPARKS fly
I shall think my thirst and hunger quelled.

If the skies tear down
I shall think them pouring for my bath.

If a hillside slide on me
I shall think it flower for my hair.

O lord white as jasmine, if my head falls from my shoulders
I shall think it your offering.

—Mahadeviyakka

God's Name

HE WHO utters the Name of God while walking
>   gets the merit of a sacrifice at every step.
His body becomes a place of pilgrimage.
He who repeats God's Name while working
>   always finds perfect peace.
He who utters the Name of God while eating
>   gets the merit of a fast
>   even though he has taken his meals.
Even if one were to give in charity
>   the whole earth encircled by the seas
>   it would not equal the merit of repeating the Name.
By the power of the Name
>   one will know what cannot be known,
One will see what cannot be seen,
One will speak what cannot be spoken,
One will meet what cannot be met.
Tuka says,
>   Incalculable is the gain that comes
>   from repeating the Name of God.

—*Tukaram*

Money's No Good Here

Sister,
I went into market
and picked up the Dark One.
You whisper
as though it were shameful,
I strike my drum and declare it in public.
You say I paid high,
I say I weighed it out on the scales,
it was cheap.
Money's no good here,
I traded my body, I paid with my life!
Dark One, give Mira a glance,
we struck a bargain
   lifetimes ago.

—*Mirabai*

Who Can Discredit Me?

THE DARK ONE'S love-stain
is on her,
other ornaments
Mira sees as mere glitter.
A mark on her forehead,
a bracelet, some prayer beads,
beyond that she wears only
        her conduct.

Make up is worthless
when you've gotten truth from a teacher.
O the Dark One has
stained me with love,
and for that some revile me,
others give honor.
I simply wander the road of the sadhus
        lost in my songs.

Never stealing,
injuring no one,
who can discredit me?
Do you think I'd step down from an elephant
to ride on the haunch
        of an ass?

—*Mirabai*

Deep into the Night

O BELOVED,
        Let us go to that place,
        Let us go there together.

Tell me, what should I wear?—
        A golden sari
        with a yellow flower behind my ear?
Or shall it be a simple dress
        with a string of pearls
        along the part of my hair?

Let me be your handmaid.
I will plant myself in your garden
        and there I will look upon your face
        and sing your praises forever.
Let me be your servant
        and let my only wages
        be the sweetness of your Name.

I have dreamt of you
        since the world began,
With a crown of peacock feathers on your head,
With robes of amber and yellow.
I see a garland of roses around your neck
        as you take the cows out to graze.

O Krishna,
        Charmer of hearts,
        Lifter of mountains,

I hear your flute calling me—
Shall I come by the secret path
    through the tall grass?

O Lord of Heavenly Blue,
My heart cannot rest until we are together,
    until we walk along the banks of the Jamuna
    deep into the night.

—Mirabai

The Swing of Consciousness

BETWEEN THE pillars of spirit and matter
    the mind has put up a swing.
There swings the bound soul and all the worlds
    with not even the slightest rest.
The sun and moon also swing,
    and there is no end to it.
The soul swings through millions of births
    like the endless circling of the sun and moon.
Billions of ages have passed
    with no sigh of relief.
The earth and sky swing,
Wind and water swing,
Taking a body, God Himself swings.

Kabir, the servant of God,
has seen it all.
O brother seekers!
Only while you are alive is there hope of finding Him.
While you are alive, meditate.
While you are alive, contemplate.
Only while you are alive can liberation be found.

If you do not cut the noose of your *karma* while living,
    what hope is there of liberation when you are dead?
It is a hopeless dream
    to think that union will come
    after the soul leaves the body.

What you get now
        is what you get then—
Otherwise, all you get is a stay in hell.
Embrace the real,
Recognize the true Guru,
Have faith in the power of the Name!
Kabir says,
        "Only spiritual practice will get you across;
        be addicted to this practice."

                                    —*Kabir*

The Simple Union

O Sadhu! the simple union is the best.

Since the day when I met with my Lord, there has been no
  end to the sport of our love.

I shut not my eyes, I close not my ears, I do not mortify my
  body;

I see with eyes open and smile, and behold His beauty
  everywhere:

I utter His Name, and whatever I see, it reminds me of
  Him; whatever I do, it becomes His worship.

The rising and the setting are one to me; all contradictions
  are solved.

Wherever I go, I move round him,

All I achieve is His service:

When I lie down, I lie prostrate at His feet.

He is the only adorable one to me: I have none other.

My tongue has left off impure words, it sings His glory day
  and night:

Whether I rise or sit down, I can never forget Him; for the
  rhythm of His music beats in my ears.

Kabir says: "My heart is frenzied, and I disclose in my soul
  what is hidden. I am immersed in that one great bliss
  which transcends all pleasure and pain."

—*Kabir*

A Country Fair for Those Mad with Love

DRIVE ME out of my mind, O Mother!
What use is esoteric knowledge
    or philosophical discrimination?
Transport me totally with the burning wine
    of your all-embracing love.
Mother of Mystery, who imbues with mystery
    the hearts of those who love you,
immerse me irretrievably
    in the stormy ocean without boundary,
pure love, pure love, pure love.

Wherever your lovers reside
    appears like a madhouse
to common perception.
Some are laughing with your freedom,
others weep tears of your tenderness,
still others dance, whirling with your bliss.
Even your devoted Gautama, Moses,
Krishna, Jesus, Nanak, and Muhammad
    are lost in the rapture of pure love.

This poet stammers,
overcome with longing:
"When? When? When?
When will I be granted companionship
    with her intense lovers?"

Their holy company is heavenly,
a country fair for those mad with love,
where every distinction
        between master and disciple
disappears.

This lover of love sings:
"Mother! Mother! Mother!
Who can fathom your mystery,
your eternal play of love with love?
You are divine madness, O goddess,
your love the brilliant crown of madness.
Please make this poor poet madly wealthy
        with the infinite treasure of your love."

                                —*Ramprasad*

I'm Going to Plunge Anyway

SOMEHOW the time will pass.
Today is going to pass,
Only your story will live,
Your name, Tara, dirtied by Your cruelty.
I come here to this marketplace
And, sold out, wait at the landing.
Mother, the sun is dying. I need a boat,
And this boatman takes only those who can pay.
He demands money
But where will a poor man get it?

Prasad cries: Woman of Stone,
Glance back and give me a seat.
I'm going to plunge anyway, singing
Your greatness, into the sea of the world.

—*Ramprasad*

Cut This Black Snarl

I'M SWEATING like the slave of an evil spirit,
Flat broke, a coolie working for nothing,
A ditch digger, and my body eats the profits.
Five Elements, Six Passions, Ten Senses—
Count them—all scream for attention.
They won't listen. I'm done for.
A blind man clutches the cane he's lost
Like a fanatic. So I clutch You, Mother,
But with my bungled karma, can't hold on.

Prasad cries out: Mother, cut this black snarl
Of acts, cut through it. Let life, when death
Closes down, shoot rejoicing up
Out of my head like a rocket.

—*Ramprasad*

Abandon Whatever Limits You Cling To

KALI IS naked reality.
She is the feminine principle, unifying wisdom.
This simpleminded lover of truth
    calls her *my Mother, my Mother,*
because she is the inexhaustible affection
    who never neglects her children,
no matter how heedless or rebellious they may be.

Wisdom Mother cares for this child
    more tenderly than human mother,
yet her creative and destructive actions
    are startling, wild, unpredictable
as those of a mad person.
She is surrounded by swirling energy,
manifest in various feminine forms
    as human beings and etheric beings:
powerful women warriors, peaceful contemplatives,
terrifying protectresses surrounded by flames.
Godhead in its three aspects,
Creator, Sustainer, and Revealer,
stands humbly before my Mother
She is supreme.

This poet urges every human heart:
"If you wish to be liberated from oppression,

abandon whatever limits you cling to
    and meditate on the limitless one
who wears limitation as a garland of heads
    severed by her sword of nondual wisdom."

                    —*Ramprasad*

I Would Not Even Care to
Be an Emperor

MOTHER OF the Universe,
I have no desire to exercise power.
I would not even care to be an emperor.
Sweet Mother, please grant me
        two simple meals each day
and wealth enough to thatch the palm roof
        of my clean earthen house,
where I offer dreaming and waking
        as red flowers at your feet.

My green village dwelling is the abode
        of your golden radiance, O Goddess.
What need have I for more elaborate construction?
If you surround me with the complex architecture
        of stature and possession,
I will refuse to call you *Mother* ever again.

O Kali, give me just enough to serve lovingly
        whatever guests may visit me.
Plain metal plates and cups will do.
Daily existence in the heart of my extended family
        is the worship beyond worship
that perceives Mother Reality
        as every being, every situation, every breath.

I will never leave this natural way of life
        to become a stern ascetic

or a teacher honored by the world.
There is only one longing this poet's soul
      declares over and over:
"Mother! Mother! Mother!
May every moment of my existence
      merge completely with your essence."

—Ramprasad

I Am Buried in Shyam

WHATEVER THE ELDERS at home may say
I can never leave my treasure, my Shyam,
His beauty and charm have eaten my heart.
I constantly fear that someone will come
And cut my ribs open to take them away.
Forever I am conscious, awake day and night,
Even when in lassitude I close my eyes.
I am buried in Shyam, the shape of my loves.

Who could ever wish me to leave my loving,
I would rather eat poison than hear such words.
I have explored his beauty and found no shores,
But the god at last is standing by me.
I will fulfill my dream and let the rest go.

—Chandidas

Turned to Gold

As the man and the woman in me
unite in love,
the brilliant beauty
balanced on the two-petalled lotus
within me
dazzles my eyes.
The rays
outshine the moon
and the jewels
glowing on the hoods of snakes.

My skin and bone
are turned to gold.
I am the reservoir of love
alive as the waves.
A single drop of water
has grown into a sea,
unnavigable.

—*Lalan*

Snared by the Beauty

My soul cries out,
snared by the beauty
of the formless one.
As I cry by myself,
night and day,
beauty amassed before my eyes
surpasses numberless moons and suns.
If I look at the clouds in the sky,
I see his beauty afloat;
and I see him walk on the stars
blazing my heart.

—*Fikirchand*

Truth Is One

PEOPLE WORSHIP GOD according to their tastes and temperaments. The mother cooks the same fish differently for her children, that each one may have what suits his stomach. For some she cooks the rich dish of pilau. But not all the children can digest it. For those with weak stomachs she prepares soup. Some, again, like fried fish or pickled fish. It depends on one's taste . . .

I see people who talk about religion constantly quarreling with one another. Hindus, Mussulmans [Muslims], Brahmos, Shaktas, Vaishnavas, Shaivas all quarrel with one another. They haven't the intelligence to understand that He who is called Krishna is also Shiva and the Primal Shakti, and that it is He, again, who is called Jesus and Allah. "There is only one Rama and He has a thousand names."

Truth is one; only It is called by different names. All people are seeking the same Truth; the variance is due to climate, temperament, and name. A lake has many ghats. From one ghat the Hindus take water in jars and call it *jal*. From another ghat the Mussulmans take water in leather bags and call it *pani*. From a third the Christians take the same thing and call it "water." Suppose someone says that the thing is not *jal* but *pani*, or that it is not *pani* but water, or that it is not water but *jal*. It would indeed be ridiculous. But this very thing is at the root of the friction among sects, their misunderstandings and quarrels. This is why people injure and kill one another, and shed blood, in the name of religion. But this is not good. Everyone is going toward God. They will all realize Him if they have sincerity and longing of heart.

—*Ramakrishna*

The Chameleon

DEVOTEE: Sir, why are there so many different opinions about God's nature? Some say that God has form, while others say that He is formless. Again, those who speak of God with form tell us about His different forms. Why all this controversy?

RAMAKRISHNA: A devotee thinks of God as he sees Him. In reality there is no confusion about God. God explains all this to the devotee if the devotee only somehow realizes Him. You haven't set your foot in that direction. How can you expect to know all about God?

Listen to a story. Once a man entered a jungle and saw a small animal on a tree. He came back and told another man that he had seen a creature of a beautiful red color on a certain tree. The second man replied: "When I went into the jungle I too saw that animal. But why do you call it red? It is green." Another man who was present contradicted them both and insisted that it was yellow. Presently others arrived and contended that it was grey, violet, blue, and so forth and so on. At last they started quarreling among themselves. To settle the dispute they all went to the tree. They saw a man sitting under it. On being asked, he replied: "Yes, I live under this tree and I know the animal very well. All your descriptions are true. Sometimes it appears red, sometimes yellow, and at other times blue, violet, grey, and so forth. It is a chameleon. And sometimes it has no color at all. Now it has a color, and now it has none."

In like manner, one who constantly thinks of God can know His real nature; he alone knows that God reveals Himself to seekers in various forms and aspects. God has attributes; then again He has none. Only the man who lives under the tree knows that the chameleon can appear in various colors, and he knows, further, that at times it has no color at all. It is the others who suffer from the agony of futile argument.

Kabir used to say, "The formless Absolute is my Father, and God with form is my Mother." God reveals Himself in the form which His devotee loves most. His love for the devotee knows no bounds.

- *Ramakrishna*

Who Weeps for God?

PEOPLE SHED a whole jug of tears for wife and children. They swim in tears for money. But who weeps for God? Cry to Him with a real cry.

Longing is like the rosy dawn. After the dawn out comes the sun. Longing is followed by the vision of God.

God reveals Himself to a devotee who feels drawn to Him by the combined force of these three attractions: the attraction of worldly possessions for the worldly man, the child's attraction for its mother, and the husband's attraction for the chaste wife. If one feels drawn to him by the combined force of these three attractions, then one can attain him.

The point is to love God even as the mother loves her child, the chaste wife her husband, and the worldly man his wealth. Join together these three forces of love, these three powers of attraction, and direct them all to God. Then you will certainly see him.

It is necessary to pray to Him with a longing heart. The kitten knows only how to call its mother, crying, "Mew, mew!" It remains satisfied wherever its mother puts it. And the mother cat puts the kitten sometimes in the kitchen, sometimes on the floor, and sometimes on the bed. When it suffers it cries only, "Mew, mew!" That's all it knows. But as soon as the mother hears this cry, wherever she may be, she comes to the kitten.

—*Ramakrishna*

How to Live in the World

A DEVOTEE who can call on God while living a house-holder's life is a hero indeed. God thinks: "He who has renounced the world for My sake will surely pray to Me; he must serve Me. Is there anything very remarkable about it? People will cry shame on him if he fails to do so. But he is blessed indeed who prays to Me in the midst of his worldly duties. He is trying to find Me, overcoming a great obstacle—pushing away, as it were, a huge block of stone weighing a ton. Such a man is a real hero."

Live in the world like an ant. The world contains a mixture of truth and untruth, sugar and sand. Be an ant and take the sugar.

Again, the world is a mixture of milk and water, the bliss of God-Consciousness and the pleasure of sense enjoyment. Be a swan and drink the milk, leaving the water aside.

Live in the world like a waterfowl. The water clings to the bird, but the bird shakes it off. Live in the world like a mudfish. The fish lives in the mud, but its skin is always bright and shiny.

The world is indeed a mixture of truth and make-believe. Discard the make-believe and take the truth.

—*Ramakrishna*

The Mother

THE DIVINE MOTHER revealed to me in the Kali temple that it was She who had become everything. She showed me that everything was full of Consciousness. The Image was Consciousness, the altar was Consciousness, the water-vessels were Consciousness, the door-sill was Consciousness, the marble floor was Consciousness—all was Consciousness.

I found everything inside the room soaked, as it were, in Bliss—the Bliss of Satchidananda. I saw a wicked man in front of the Kali temple; but in him also I saw the Power of the Divine Mother vibrating.

That was why I fed a cat with the food that was to be offered to the Divine Mother. I clearly perceived that the Divine Mother Herself had become everything—even the cat.

Whatever we see or think about is the manifestation of the Mother, of the Primordial Energy, the Primal Consciousness. Creation, preservation, and destruction, living beings and the universe, and further, meditation and the meditator, *bhakti* [devotion] and *prema* [divine love]—all these are manifestations of the glory of that Power. . . .

Brahman, the Godhead, and Shakti, the Primal Energy, are like the snake and its wriggling motion. Thinking of the snake, one must think of its wriggling motion, and thinking of the wriggling motion, one must think of the snake. Or they are like milk and its whiteness. Thinking of milk one has to think of its color, that is, whiteness, and thinking of the whiteness of milk, one has to think of milk itself. Or they are like water and its wetness. Thinking of water, one has to think of its wetness, and thinking of the wetness of water, one has to think of water. . . .

The Primordial Power is ever at play. She is creating, preserving, and destroying in play, as it were. This power is called Kali. Kali is . . . Brahman and Brahman is . . . Kali. It is one and the same Reality. When we think of It as inactive, that is to say, not engaged in the acts of creation, preservation, and destruction, then we call it Brahman. But when It engages in these activities, then we call it Kali or Shakti. The Reality is one and the same; the difference is in name and form. . . .

A man once saw the image of the Divine Mother wearing a sacred thread. He said to the worshiper: "What? You have put the sacred thread on the Mother's neck!" The worshiper said: "Brother, I see that you have truly known the Mother. But I have not yet been able to find out whether She is male or female; that is why I have put the sacred thread on Her image."

That which is Shakti is also Brahman. That which has form, again, is without form. That which has attributes, again, has no attributes. Brahman is Shakti; Shakti is Brahman. They are not two. These are only two aspects, male and female, of the same Reality, Existence-Knowledge-Bliss Absolute.

—*Ramakrishna*

Perfect Awareness

THE *paramahamsa* [awakened being] is like a five-year-old child. He sees everything filled with Consciousness. At one time I was staying at Kamarpukur when Shivaram, my nephew, was four or five years old. One day he was trying to catch grasshoppers near the pond. The leaves were moving. To stop their rustling he said to the leaves: "Hush! Hush! I want to catch a grasshopper." Another day it was stormy. It rained hard. Shivaram was with me inside the house. There were flashes of lightning. He wanted to open the door and go out. I scolded him and stopped him, but still he peeped out now and then. When he saw the lightning he exclaimed, "There, uncle! They are striking matches again!"

The *paramahamsa* is like a child. He cannot distinguish between a stranger and a relative. He isn't particular about worldly relationships. One day Shivaram said to me, "Uncle, are you my father's brother or his brother-in-law?" . . .

Sometimes the *paramahamsa* behaves like a madman. When I experienced that divine madness I used to worship my own sexual organ as the Shiva-phallus [Shiva-*lingam*]. But I can't do that now. A few days after the dedication of the temple at Dakshineswar, a madman came there who was really a sage endowed with the Knowledge of Brahman. He had a bamboo twig in one hand and a potted mango-plant in the other, and was wearing torn shoes. He didn't follow any social conventions. After bathing in the Ganges he didn't perform any religious rites. He ate something that he carried in a corner of his wearing-cloth. Then he entered the Kali temple and chanted hymns to the Deity. The temple trembled. . . . The madman wasn't allowed to eat at the guest-house, but he paid no attention to this slight. He searched for food in the rubbish heap where the dogs were eating crumbs from the discarded leaf-plates. Now and then he pushed the dogs aside to get his crumbs. The dogs didn't mind either. Haladhari followed him and asked: "Who are you? Are you a *purnajnani* [a perfect knower of Brahman]?" The madman whispered, "Sh! Yes, I am a *purnajnani*." Haladhari followed him a great way when he left the garden. After passing the gate he said to Haladhari: "What else shall I say to you? When you no longer make any distinction between the water of this pool and the water of the Ganges, then you will know that you have Perfect Knowledge." Saying this he walked rapidly away.

—*Ramakrishna*

Worship the Living God

We WANT to worship a living God. I have not seen anything but God all my life, nor have you. To see this chair you first see God, and then the chair in and through Him. He is everywhere, saying, "I am." The moment you feel "I am," you are conscious of Existence. Where shall we go to find God if we cannot see Him in our own hearts and in every living being? "Thou art the man, Thou art the woman, Thou art the girl, and Thou art the boy. Thou art the old man tottering with a stick. Thou art the young man walking in the pride of his strength. Thou art all that exists"—a wonderful living God, who is the only fact in the universe.

This seems to many to be a terrible contradiction of the traditional God, who lives behind a veil somewhere and whom nobody ever sees. The priests only give us an assurance that if we follow them, listen to their admonitions, and walk in the way they mark out for us, then, when we die, they will give us a passport to enable us to see the face of God! What are all these heaven ideas but simply modifications of this nonsensical priestcraft?

Of course, the impersonal idea is very destructive; it takes away all trade from the priests, churches, and temples. In India there is a famine now, but there are temples in each one of which there are jewels worth a king's ransom! If the priests taught this Impersonal idea to the people, their occupation would be gone. Yet we have to teach it unselfishly, without priestcraft. You are God and so am I. Who obeys whom? Who worships whom? You are the highest temple of God. I would rather worship you than any temple, image, or Bible. Why are some people so contradictory in their thought? They are like fish slipping through our fingers. They say they are hard-headed, practical men. Very good. But what is more practical than worshipping here, worshipping you? I see you, feel you, and I know you are God. The Mohammedan says there is no God but Allah. Vedanta says there is nothing that is not God. It may frighten many of you, but you will understand it by degrees. The living God is within you, and yet you are building churches and temples and believing all sorts of imaginary nonsense. The only God to worship is the human soul in the human body. Of course all animals are temples too, but man is the highest, the Taj Mahal of temples. If I cannot worship in that, no other temple will be of any advantage. The moment I have realized God sitting in the temple of every human body, the moment I stand in reverence before every human being and see God in him, that moment I am free from bondage. Everything that binds vanishes, and I am free.

—*Vivekananda*

All Gods Are in You

IN WORSHIPPING GOD we have been always worshipping our own hidden Self. The worst lie that you can ever tell yourself is that you were born a sinner or a wicked man. Suppose there is a baby here, and you place a bag of gold on the table. Suppose a robber comes and takes the gold away. To the baby it is all the same; because there is no robber inside, so he sees no robber outside. To sinners and vile men there is vileness outside, but not to good men. So the wicked see this universe as a hell, and the partially good see it as heaven, while the perfect beings realize it as God Himself. Only when a man sees this universe as God does the veil fall from his eyes; then that man, purified and cleansed, finds his whole vision changed. The bad dreams that have been torturing him for millions of years all vanish, and he who was thinking of himself as either a man or a god or a demon, he who was thinking of himself as living in low places, in high places, on earth, in heaven, and so on, finds that he is really omnipresent; that all time is in him, and that he is not in time; that all the heavens are in him, that he is not in any heaven; and that all the gods that man ever worshipped are in him, and that he is not in any one of those gods. He was the manufacturer of gods and demons, of men and plants and animals and stones. And the real nature of man now stands unfolded to him as being higher than heaven, more perfect than this universe of ours, more infinite than infinite time, more omnipresent than the omnipresent ether.

—*Vivekananda*

The Supreme Worship

İT IS IN LOVE that religion exists and not in ceremony—in the pure and sincere love in the heart. Unless a man is pure in body and mind, his coming into a temple and worshipping Shiva is useless. The prayers of those who are pure in mind and body will be answered by Shiva, and those who are impure and yet try to teach religion to others will fail in the end. External worship is only a symbol of internal worship, but internal worship and purity are the real things. Without them, external worship would be of no avail.

This is the gist of all worship: to be pure and to do good to others. He who sees Shiva in the poor, in the weak, and in the diseased, really worships Shiva. And if he sees Shiva only in the image, his worship is but preliminary. He who has served and helped one poor man seeing Shiva in him, without thinking of his caste or creed or race or anything, with him Shiva is more pleased than with the man who sees Him only in temples.

A rich man had a garden and two gardeners. One of these gardeners was very lazy and did not work. But when the owner came to the garden the lazy man would get up and fold his arms and say, "How beautiful is the face of my master," and dance before him. The other gardener would not talk much, but would work hard and produce all sorts of fruits and vegetables, which he would carry on his head to his master, who lived a long way off. Of these two gardeners, which would be the more beloved of his master? Shiva is that master and this world is His garden, and there are two sorts of gardeners here—the one who is lazy, hypocritical, and does nothing, only talking about Shiva's beautiful eyes and nose and other features, and the other, who is taking care of Shiva's children, all those who are poor and weak, all animals, and all His creation. Which of these would be the more beloved of Shiva? Certainly he who serves His children. He who wants to serve the father must serve the children first. He who wants to serve Shiva must serve His children—must serve all creatures in this world first. It is said in the shastra [the scriptures] that those who serve the servants of God are His greatest servants. So you will bear this in mind.

—*Vivekananda*

The Open Secret

NONE CAN DIE. None can be degraded forever. Life is but a playground, however gross the play may be. However we may receive blows and however knocked about we may be, the Soul is there and is never injured. We are that Infinite.

Thus sang a Vedantist: "I never had fear or doubt. Death never came to me. I never had a father or mother, for I was never born. Where are my foes?—for I am All. I am Existence, Knowledge, Bliss Absolute. I am It. I am It."

However much the body rebels, however much the mind rebels, in the midst of uttermost darkness, in the midst of agonizing tortures, in uttermost despair, repeat this once, twice, thrice, evermore. Light comes gently, slowly, but surely it comes.

Many times I have been in the jaws of death, starving, footsore, and weary. For days and days I had no food, and often could walk no farther. I would sink down under a tree, and life would seem to be ebbing away. I could not speak. I could scarcely think. But at last the mind reverted to the idea: "I have no fear of death. I never hunger or thirst. I am It! I am It! The whole of nature cannot crush me—it is my servant. Assert thy strength, thou Lord of lords and God of gods! Regain thy lost empire! Arise and walk and stop not!" And I would rise up, reinvigorated, and here am I, living, today. Thus, whenever darkness comes, assert the reality and everything adverse must vanish. For, after all, it is but a dream. Mountain high though the difficulties appear, terrible and gloomy though all things seem, they are but maya. Fear not—it is banished. Crush it and it vanishes. Stamp upon it and it dies. Be not afraid. Think not how many times you fail. Never mind—time is infinite. Go forward. Assert yourself again and again and light must come.

—*Vivekananda*

The Sickbed-21

WHEN I WOKE up this morning
There was a rose in my flower-vase:
The question came to me—
The power that brought you through cyclic time
To final beauty,
Dodging at every turn
The torment of ugly incompleteness,
Is it blind, is it abstracted,
Does it, like a world-denying *sannyasi*,
Make no distinction between beauty and the opposite
    of beauty?
Is it merely rational,
Merely physical,
Lacking in sensibility?
There are some who argue
That grace and ugliness take equal seats
At the court of Creation,
That neither is refused entry
By the guards.
As a poet I cannot enter such arguments—
I can only gaze at the universe
In its full, true form,
At the millions of stars in the sky
Carrying their huge harmonious beauty—
Never breaking their rhythm
Or losing their tune,
Never deranged

And never stumbling—
I can only gaze and see, in the sky,
The spreading layers
Of a vast, radiant, petalled rose.

                    —*Rabindranath Tagore*

The Nature of Mind: Who Am I?

What is the nature of the mind?

What is called "mind" is a wondrous power residing in the Self. It causes all thought to arise. Apart from thoughts, there is no such thing as mind. Therefore, thought is the nature of mind. Apart from thoughts, there is no independent entity called the world. In deep sleep there are no thoughts, and there is no world. In the states of waking and dream, there are thoughts, and there is a world also. Just as the spider emits the thread [of the web] out of itself and again withdraws it into itself, likewise the mind projects the world out of itself and again resolves it into itself. When the mind comes out of the Self, the world appears. Therefore, when the world appears (to be real), the Self does not appear; and when the Self appears [shines] the world does not appear. When one persistently inquires into the nature of the mind, the mind will end leaving the Self [as the residue]. What is referred to as the Self is the *Atman*. The mind always exists only in dependence on something gross; it cannot stay alone. It is the mind that is called the subtle body or the soul (*jiva*).

What is the path of inquiry for understanding the nature of the mind?

That which rises as "I" in this body is the mind. If one inquires as to where in the body the thought "I" rises first, one would discover that it rises in the heart. That is the place of the mind's origin. Even if one thinks constantly "I," "I," one will be led to that place. Of all the thoughts that arise in the mind, the "I" thought is the first. It is only after the rise of this that the other thoughts arise. It is after the appearance of the first personal pronoun that the second and third personal pronouns appear; without the first personal pronoun there will not be the second and third.

How will the mind become quiescent?

By the inquiry "Who am I?" The thought "who am I?" will destroy all other thoughts, and like the stick used for stirring the burning pyre, it will itself in the end get destroyed. Then, there will arise Self-realization.

What is the means for constantly holding on to the thought "Who am I?"?

When other thoughts arise, one should not pursue them, but should inquire: "To whom did they arise?" It does not matter how many thoughts arise. As each thought arises, one should inquire with diligence, "To whom has this thought arisen?" The answer that would emerge would be "To me." Thereupon if one inquires "Who am I?," the mind will go back to its source; and the thought that arose will become quiescent. With repeated practice in this manner, the mind will develop the skill to stay in its source. When the mind that is subtle goes out through the brain and the sense-organs, the gross names and forms appear; when it stays in the heart, the names and forms disappear. Not letting the mind go out but retaining it in the Heart is what is called "inwardness (*antar-mukha*). Letting the mind to go out of the Heart is known as "externalization" (*bahir-mukha*). Thus, when the mind stays in the Heart, the "I" which is the source of all thoughts will go, and the Self which ever exists will shine. Whatever one does, one should do without the egoity "I." If one acts in that way, all will appear as of the nature of Shiva (God).

—*Ramana Maharshi*

The Self and the Cinema

How can there be a connection between the Self which is pure knowledge and the triple factors which are relative knowledge?

This is, in a way, like the working of a cinema as shown below:—

Cinema Show	Self
(1) The lamp inside (the apparatus)	(1) The Self
(2) The lens in front of the lamp	(2) The pure (*satvic*) mind close to the Self
(3) The film, which is a long series of separate photos	(3) The stream of latent tendencies consisting of subtle thoughts
(4) The lens, the light passing through it, and the lamp, which together form the focused light	(4) The mind, the illumination of it and the Self, which together form the seer or the *jiva*
(5) The light passing through the lens and falling on the screen	(5) The light of the Self emerging from the mind through the senses and falling on the world

(6)	The various kinds of pictures appearing in the light of the screen	(6)	The various forms and names appearing as the objects perceived in the light of the world
(7)	The mechanism which sets the film in motion	(7)	The divine law manifesting the latent tendencies of the mind

Just as the pictures appear on the screen as long as the film throws the shadows through the lens, so the phenomenal world will continue to appear to the individual in the waking and dream states as long as there are latent mental impressions. Just as the lens magnifies the tiny specks on the film to a huge size and as a number of pictures are shown in a second, so the mind enlarges the sproutlike tendencies into treelike thoughts and shows in a second innumerable worlds. Again, just as there is only the light of the lamp visible when there is no film, so the Self alone shines without the triple factors when the mental concepts in the form of tendencies are absent in the states of deep sleep, swoon, and *samadhi*. Just as the lamp illumines the lens, etc., while remaining unaffected, the Self illumines the ego, while remaining unaffected.

—*Ramana Maharshi*

I Am a Child

I AM NOW seventy-four years old. And yet I feel that I am an infant. I feel clearly that in spite of all the changes I am a child. My Guru told me; that child, which is you even now, is your real self. Go back to that state of pure being, where the "I am" is still in its purity before it got contaminated with "this I am" or "that I am." Your burden is of false self-identifications—abandon them all. My Guru told me—"Trust me. I tell you; you are divine. Take it as the absolute truth. Your joy is divine, your suffering is divine too. All comes from God. Remember it always. You are God, your will alone is done." I did believe him and soon realized how wonderfully true and accurate were his words. I did not condition my mind by thinking: "I am God, I am wonderful, I am beyond." I simply followed his instruction, which was to focus the mind on pure being "I am," and stay in it. I used to sit for hours together, with nothing but the "I am" in my mind and soon peace and joy and a deep all-embracing love became my normal state. In it all disappeared—myself, my Guru, the life lived, the world around me. Only peace remained and unfathomable silence.

—*Nisargadatta Maharaj*

The Divine Mother

THERE ARE three ways of being of the Mother of which you can become aware when you enter into touch of oneness with the Conscious Force that upholds us and the universe. Transcendent, the original supreme Shakti, she stands above the worlds and links the creation to the ever unmanifest mystery of the Supreme. Universal, the cosmic Mahashakti, she creates all these beings and contains and enters, supports and conducts all these million processes and forces. Individual, she embodies the power of these two vaster ways of her existence, makes them living and near to us, and mediates between the human personality and the divine Nature.

The one original transcendent Shakti, the Mother stands above all the worlds and bears in her eternal consciousness the Supreme Divine. Alone, she harbors the absolute Power and the ineffable Presence; containing or calling the Truths that have to be manifested, she brings them down from the Mystery in which they were hidden into the light of her infinite consciousness and gives them a form of force in her omnipotent power and her boundless life and a body in the universe. . . .

All is her play with the Supreme; all is her manifestation of the mysteries of the Eternal, the miracles of the Infinite. All is she, for all are parcel and portion of the divine Conscious-Force. Nothing can be, here or elsewhere, but what she decides and the Supreme sanctions; nothing can take shape except what she, moved by the Supreme, perceives and forms after casting it into seed in her creating Ananda.

The Mahashakti, the universal Mother, works out whatever is transmitted by her transcendent consciousness from the Supreme and enters into the worlds that she has made; her presence fills and supports them with the divine spirit and the divine all-sustaining force and delight without which they could not exist. That which we call Nature or Prakriti is only her most outward executive aspect; she marshals and arranges the harmony of her forces and processes, impels the operations of Nature, and moves among them secret or manifest in all that can be seen or experienced or put into motion of life. Each of the worlds is nothing but one play of the Mahashakti of that system of worlds or universe, who is there as the cosmic Soul and Personality of the transcendent Mother. Each is something that she has seen in her vision, gathered into her heart of beauty and power and created in her Ananda.

—*Sri Aurobindo*

All for Her

If you want to be a true doer of divine works, your first aim must be to be totally free from all desire and self-regarding ego. All your life must be an offering and a sacrifice to the Supreme; your only object in action shall be to serve, to receive, to fulfill, to become a manifesting instrument of the Divine Shakti in her works. You must grow in the divine consciousness till there is no difference between your will and hers, no motive except her impulsion in you, no action that is not her conscious action in you and through you.

Until you are capable of this complete dynamic identification, you have to regard yourself as a soul and body created for her service, one who does all for her sake. Even if the idea of the separate worker is strong in you and you feel that it is you who do the act, yet it must be done for her. All stress of egoistic choice, all hankering after personal profit, all stipulation of self-regarding desire must be extirpated from the nature. There must be no demand for fruit and no seeking for reward; the only fruit for you is the pleasure of the Divine Mother and the fulfillment of her work, your only reward a constant progression in divine consciousness and calm and strength and bliss. The joy of service and the joy of inner growth through works is the sufficient recompense of the selfless worker.

But a time will come when you will feel more and more that you are the instrument and not the worker. For first by the force of your devotion your contact with the Divine Mother will become so intimate that at all times you will have only to concentrate and to put everything into her hands to have her present guidance, her direct command or impulse, the sure indication of the thing to be done, and the way to do it and the result. And afterward you will realize that the divine Shakti not only inspires and guides, but initiates and carries out your works; all your movements are originated by her, all your powers are hers, mind, life, and body are conscious and joyful instruments of her action, means for her play, molds for her manifestation in the physical universe. There can be no more happy condition than this union and dependence; for this step carries you back beyond the borderline from the life of stress and suffering in the ignorance into the truth of your spiritual being, into its deep peace and its intense Ananda.

While this transformation is being done it is more than ever necessary to keep yourself free from all taint of the perversions of the ego. Let no demand or insistence creep in to stain the purity of the self-giving and the sacrifice. There must be no attachment to the work or the result, no laying down of conditions, no claim to possess the Power that should possess you, no pride of the instrument, no vanity or arrogance. Nothing in the mind or in the vital or physical parts should be suffered to distort to its own use or seize for its own personal and separate satisfaction the greatness of the forces that are acting through you. Let your faith, your sincerity, your purity of aspiration be absolute and pervasive of all the planes and layers of the being; then every disturbing element and distorting influence will progressively fall away from your nature.

The last stage of this perfection will come when you are completely identified with the Divine Mother and feel yourself to be no longer another and separate being, instrument, servant, or worker but truly a child and eternal portion of her consciousness and force. Always she will be in you and you in her; it will be your constant, simple and natural experience that all your thought and seeing and action, your very breathing or moving come from her and are hers. You will know and see and feel that you are a person and power formed by her out of herself, put out from her for the play and yet always safe in her, being of her being, consciousness of her consciousness, force of her force, Ananda of her Ananda. When this condition is entire and her supramental energies can freely move you, then you will be perfect in divine works; knowledge, will, action will become sure, simple, luminous, spontaneous, flawless, an outflow from the Supreme, a divine movement of the Eternal.

—Sri Aurobindo

The Supramental Force

HERE THE evolution takes place in a material universe; the foundation, the original substance, the first established all-conditioning status of things is Matter. Mind and Life are evolved in Matter, but they are limited and modified in their action by the obligation to use its substance for their instrumentation and by their subjection to the law of material Nature even while they modify what they undergo and use. . . .

An original creative or evolutionary Power there must be; but, although Matter is the first substance, the original and ultimate Power is not an inconscient material Energy; for then life and consciousness would be absent, since Inconscience cannot evolve consciousness nor an inanimate Force evolve life. There must be, therefore, since Mind and Life also are not that, a secret Consciousness greater than Life-Consciousness or Mind-Consciousness, an Energy more essential than the material Energy. Since it is greater than Mind, it must be a supramental Consciousness-Force; since it is a power of essential substance other than Matter, it must be the power of that which is the supreme essence and substance of all things, a power of the Spirit. There is a creative energy of Mind and a creative Life-Force, but they are instrumental and partial, not original and decisive: Mind and Life do indeed modify the material substance they inhabit and its energies and are not merely determined by them, but the extent and way of this material modification and determination are fixed by the inhabitant and all-containing Spirit through a secret indwelling light and force of Supermind, an occult gnosis—an invisible self-knowledge and all-knowledge. If there is to be an entire transformation, it can only be by the full emergence of the law of the Spirit; its power of Supermind or gnosis must have entered into Matter and it must evolve in Matter. It must change the mental into the supramental being, make the inconscient in us conscious, spiritualize our material substance, erect its law of gnostic consciousness in our whole evolutionary being and nature.

—*Sri Aurobindo*

The New Being

THE MENTAL man has not been Nature's last effort or highest reach—though he has been, in general, more fully evolved in his own nature than those who have achieved themselves below or aspired above him; she has pointed man to a yet higher and more difficult level, inspired him with the ideal of a spiritual living, begun the evolution in him of a spiritual being. The spiritual man is her supreme supernormal effort of human creation; for, having evolved the mental creator, thinker, sage, prophet of an ideal, the self-controlled, self-disciplined, harmonized mental being, she has tried to go higher and deeper within and call out into the front the soul and inner mind and heart, call down from above the forces of the spiritual mind and higher mind and overmind and create under their light and by their influence the spiritual sage, seer, prophet, God-lover, Yogin, gnostic, Sufi, mystic. . . .

The spiritual man is the sign of this new evolution, this new and higher endeavor of Nature. But this evolution differs from the past process of the evolutionary Energy in two respects: it is conducted by a conscious effort of the human mind, and it is not confined to a conscious progression of the surface nature, but is accompanied by an attempt to break the walls of the Ignorance and extend ourselves inward into the secret principle of our present being and outward into cosmic being as well as upward toward a higher principle. Up till now what Nature had achieved was an enlarging of the bounds of our surface Knowledge-

Ignorance; what it attempted in the spiritual endeavor is to abolish the Ignorance, to go inward and discover the soul and to become united in consciousness with God and with all existence. This is the final aim of the mental stage of evolutionary Nature in man; it is the initial step toward a radical transmutation of the Ignorance into the Knowledge. The spiritual change begins by an influence of the inner being and the higher spiritual mind, an action felt and accepted on the surface; but this by itself can lead only to an illumined mental idealism or to the growth of a religious mind, a religious temperament or some devotion in the heart and piety in the conduct; . . . much has to be done, we have to live deeper within, we have to exceed our present consciousness and surpass our present status of Nature.

It is evident that if we can live thus deeper within and put out steadily the inner forces into the outer instrumentation or raise ourselves to dwell on higher and wider levels and bring their powers to bear on physical existence, not merely receive influences descending from them, which is all we can now do, there could begin a heightening of our force of conscious being so as to create a new principle of consciousness, a new range of activities, new values for all things, a widening of our consciousness and life, a taking up and transformation of the lower grades of our existence—in brief, the whole evolutionary process by which the Spirit in Nature creates a higher type of being.

—*Sri Aurobindo*

The New Body

THE BODY will be turned by the power of the spiritual
consciousness into a true and fit and perfectly responsive
instrument of the Spirit.

This new relation of the Spirit and the body assumes—
and makes possible—a free acceptance of the whole of material Nature in a place of rejection; the drawing back from
her, the refusal of all identification or acceptance, which is
the first normal necessity of the spiritual consciousness for
its liberation, is no longer imperative. To cease to be identified with the body, to separate oneself from the body-con-
sciousness, is a recognized and necessary step whether
toward spiritual liberation or toward spiritual perfection
and mastery over Nature. But this redemption once ef-
fected, the descent of the spiritual light and force can in-
vade and take up the body also and there can be a new
liberated and sovereign acceptance of material Nature.
That is possible, indeed, only if there is a changed commu-
nion of the Spirit with Matter, a control, a reversal of the
present balance of interaction that allows physical Nature
to veil the Spirit and affirm her own dominance. In the light
of a larger knowledge Matter also can be seen to be the
Brahman, a self-energy put forth by the Brahman, a form
and substance of Brahman; aware of the secret consciousness within material substance, secure in this larger knowledge, the gnostic light and power can unite itself with
Matter and accept it as an instrument of a spiritual manifestation . . . The Spirit has made itself Matter in order to

place itself there as an instrument for the well-being, and joy of created beings, for a self-offering of universal physical utility and service. The gnostic being, using Matter but using it without material or vital attachment or desire, will feel that he is using the Spirit in this form of itself with its consent and sanction for its own purpose. There will be in him a certain respect for physical things, an awareness of the occult consciousness in them, a worship of the Divine, the Brahman, in what he uses, a care for a perfect and faultless use of his divine material, for a true rhythm, ordered harmony, beauty in the life of Matter, in the utilization of Matter.

As a result of this new relation between the Spirit and the body, the gnostic evolution will effectuate the spiritualization, perfection and fulfillment of the physical being.

—*Sri Aurobindo*

The New Race

A SUPRAMENTAL or gnostic race of beings would not be a race made according to a single type, molded in a single fixed pattern; for the law of the Supermind is unity fulfilled in diversity, and therefore there would be an infinite diversity in the manifestation of the gnostic consciousness although that consciousness would still be one in its basis, in its constitution, in its all-revealing and all-uniting order . . . But in the supramental race itself, in the variation of its degrees, the individuals would not be cast according to a single type of individuality; each would be different from the other, a unique formation of the Being, although one with all the rest in foundation of self and sense of oneness and in the principle of his being. . . .

The gnostic individual would be the consummation of the spiritual man; his whole way of being, thinking, living, acting would be governed by the power of a vast universal spirituality. All the trinities of the Spirit would be real to his self-awareness and realized in his inner life. All his existence would be fused in oneness with the transcendent and universal Self and Spirit; all his action would originate from and obey the supreme Self and Spirit's divine governance of Nature. All life would have to him the sense of the Conscious Being, the Purusha within, finding its self-expression in Nature; his life and all its thoughts, feelings, acts would be filled for him with that significance and built upon that foundation of its reality. He would feel the presence of the Divine in every center of his consciousness, in every vibration of his life-force, in every cell of his body. In all the workings of his force of Nature he would be aware of the workings of the supreme World-Mother, the Supernature; he would see his natural being as the becoming and manifestation of the power of the World-Mother. In this consciousness he would live and act in an entire transcendent freedom, a complete joy of the Spirit, an entire identity with the cosmic Self and a spontaneous sympathy with all in the universe.

—*Sri Aurobindo*

One Single Life

THEN SHALL be ended here the Law of Pain.
Earth shall be made a home of Heaven's light. . . .
The superconscient beam shall touch men's eyes
And the truth-conscious world come down to earth
Invading matter with the Spirit's ray,
Awakening its silence to immortal thoughts,
Awakening the dumb heart to the living Word.
This mortal life shall house Eternity's bliss,
The body's self taste immortality.

O mind, grow full of the eternal peace:
O work, cry out the immortal litany:
Built is the golden tower, the flame-child born.

The supermind shall claim the world for Light
And thrill with love of God the enamored heart
And place Light's crown on Nature's lifted head
And found Light's reign on her unshaking base. . . .
A soul shall wake in the Inconscient's house;
The mind shall be God-vision's tabernacle,
The body intuition's instrument,
And life a channel for God's visible power. . . .

The Spirit's tops and Nature's base shall draw
Near to the secret of their separate truth
And know each other as one deity.

The Spirit shall look out through Matter's gaze
And Matter shall reveal the Spirit's face.
Then man and superman shall be at one
And all the earth become a single life.

—From "Savitri" by Sri Aurobindo

Glossary of Sanskrit Names and Terms

Advaita Vedanta (*advaita* = "not-two") · The metaphysical tradition of nondualism, rooted in the Upanishads. *See also* Vedanta.

Agni · God of fire in the Vedas, often involved in sacred rituals.

Arjuna ("white, bright") · The hero of the *Bhagavad Gita* and a disciple of Lord Krishna, who teaches him the meaning of life.

Asura · Demonic force.

Atman ("self") · 1. Oneself. 2. The transcendental self, identical with the absolute (Brahman).

Bauls · A sect of mystics who roam the countryside of Bengal in eastern India, singing songs to the Divine. The Baul poets embrace the influences of both Islamic Sufism and the Hindu Tantric tradition.

Brahma · God as Creator, not to be confused with Brahman, the Absolute. Brahma is one of the Hindu triad of deities known as the Trimurti. The other two are Vishnu as Preserver and Shiva as Destroyer.

Brahman (from Sanskrit *br*, "to breathe," and *brih*, "to be great") · In Advaita (nondual) Vedanta, the Absolute or transcendental ground of Being.

dharma ("sustain, support, uphold") · 1. Cosmic law or order. 2. Virtue or morality, understood as a manifestation of Divine Law. 3. Teaching or doctrine.

Indra · Great Vedic god associated with war and the sky.

Jamuna · A sacred river in North India.

jiva · The psyche, or that part of the finite human being that feels itself separate from others and is ignorant of the transcendental Self.

Kali · The "dark" Mother Goddess, killer of illusions.

karma (Sanskrit: *karman*) · The universal law of cause and effect as applied to all thoughts and actions, and source of rebirth. Liberation means, in part, freedom from past karma and the "drying up" of all illusions and desires that create new karma.

Krishna ("attractor") · An avatar, or incarnation, of Lord Vishnu. In the *Bhagavad Gita* he teaches Arjuna the laws of divine life.

kundalini ("the coiled one") · Known as the serpent power (*kundalini-shakti*) that lies coiled up at the lowest psychospiritual center (chakra) at the base of the spine. The aim of Tantrism is to awaken this power.

lingam ("sign, symbol") · In Shaivism, the worship of Shiva as the Supreme Deity, the symbol of the creative power of the Divine; the phallus as a symbol of creativity.

mantram · A combination of sacred syllables that concentrates spiritual energy and acts as a lens to focus spiritual power, enabling the mind to concentrate and transcend ordinary consciousness.

moksha ("liberation, release") · Self-Realization.

Nanak, Guru · The founder of the Sikh religion in the sixteenth century.

OM (OR *AUM*) · The key *mantram* of Hinduism, symbolizing the Absolute.

Purusha · The person, spirit, man. Both the primordial man of cosmic dimensions, hymmed in the Rig Veda, and also the "inner man" or "spiritual person" in man (as in the Upashinads).

Ramanatha · One of Shiva's sacred names.

Rudra ("Howler") · One of the earliest known epithets or forms of Shiva, often invoked in the Vedas and Upanishads.

sadhana · The path of spiritual realization.

sadhu ("good one") · A virtuous ascetic.

samadhi (nondual ecstasy) · In the Indian metaphysical systems, many different kinds of mystical ecstasy are classified, the highest being *nirvikalpa samadhi* (ecstasy beyond any idea or concept, total immersion in the Godhead) and *sahaja samadhi* (the spontaneously arising natural bliss of a sage in union with both the transcendent and the immanent Divine).

sannyasi ("renouncer") · A person who practices *sannyasa*, or renunciation; one who renounces the world and earthly possessions.

Shakti ("power") · The feminine Power of the Godhead, or Primordial Creative Energy.

Shanti ("ultimate peace") · One of the central qualities of Brahman, the Absolute.

Shiva ("benign") · The God of Destruction and Renewal, the supreme Yogi.

Shyam ("Dark One") · One of Krishna's sacred names.

Tantra (from Sanskrit *tan*, "stretch, expand") · A set of spiritual and physical exercises in Hinduism and Buddhism, designed to initiate the seeker directly into the divine ground of life, to stretch or expand his or her consciousness so that it can embrace all the levels of reality in an experience of interdependence and unity. One aspect of Tantra as practiced in ancient India was a celebration of sexuality as a way to divine initiation and ecstasy. Tantric philosophy recognized the inextricable interrelationship of soul and body, spirit and matter, transcendence and immanence, and knew that this electric dance of opposites could be experienced in all its bliss and power in the practice of a consecrated sexuality.

tapas ("glow, heat") · Ascetic practices of various kinds, designed to create in the yogi divine power and strength.

Tara ("star") · One of the sacred names of the Divine Mother, also used in Mahayana Buddhism.

turiya ("the fourth") · The consciousness of the Divine Self that includes and transcends the three consciousnesses of waking, dream, and deep sleep.

Vedanta ("end of the Vedas") · The Hindu metaphysical tradition based on the teachings of the Upanishads, concerned with the inner meaning of the Vedas. The great school of Advaita Vedanta teaches that reality is nondual.

Vishnu · God the Preserver, whose main avatars, or incarnations, are Rama and Krishna.

yoga · Spiritual or mystical practice leading to union with the Divine.

yogi · A person who practices yoga devotedly.

Contributors, Sources, and Credits

Ashtavakra Gita · An anonymous text, believed to have been composed by a follower of Shankaracharya, conveying the essential teachings of Advaita Vedanta through a dialogue between the sage Ashtavakra and his disciple, King Janaka. From *The Heart of Awareness: A translation of the* Ashtavakra Gita by Thomas Byrom, © 1990 by Thomas Byrom. Reprinted by arrangement with Shambhala Publications, Inc., Boston, *www.shambhala. com.*

Atharva Veda (from *atharvan*, "knowledge") · One of the four Vedic hymn collections, consisting mostly of magical spells, with certain important testimonies to early forms of yoga.

Aurobindo, Sri (1872–1950) · One of modern India's greatest sages. He was educated at Cambridge and wrote in English. Quoted with permission from the Sri Aurobindo Ashram Trust, Pondicherry, India.

Bhagavad Gita ("Song of the Lord") · The earliest and most celebrated of all yoga scriptures. Composed between the fifth and second centuries BCE, it forms part of the great Indian epic *Mahabharata*. Tradition claims that it was composed by the sage Vyasa through direct divine inspiration. All excerpts from the Bhagavad Gita are from *The Bhagavod Gita* translated by Eknath Easwaran,

founder of the Blue Mountain Center of Meditation,
copyright 1985; reprinted by permission of Nilgiri Press,
Tomales, California. *www.nilgiri.org.*

Brihadaranyaka Upanishad · *See* Upanishads.

Chandi Patha · A scripture of the Shakta tradition, glorify-
ing the Divine Mother. Quoted with permission from
Chandi Path, translated by Swami Satayananda Sara-
swati. Published by Devi Mandir Publications, 5950
Highway 128, Napa, CA 94558.

Chandidas (14th century) · A Bengali poet famed for his
songs celebrating the divine love of Lord Krishna and
the *gopi* (cowherd) Radha. "I am Buried in Shyam" is
from *Love Songs of Chandidas* by Deben Bhattacharya
(New South Wales, Australia: Allen & Unwin, 1963).

Chandogya Upanishad · *See* Upanishads.

Dasimayya, Devara (10th century) · One of the great poet-
saints of the Lingayat sect of Shiva-worshipers, he wrote
in Kannada, the language of Karnataka in South India.
"This Miracle" by Devara Dasimayya is from *Speaking of
Siva,* translated by A. K. Ramanujan (New York: Penguin, 1973).

Devi Gita ("Song of the Goddess") · A text of the Goddess-
worshiping Shakta sect. "The Goddess Reveals Her Cosmic Body" and "The Goddess Explains at Length the
Supreme Devotion Beyond the Gunas" are reprinted by
permission from *The Devi Gita: The Song of the Goddess:
Translation, Annotation, and Commentary* by C. Mac-
kenzie Brown, the State University of New York Press ©
1998, State University of New York. All rights reserved.

Fikirchand (19th century) · A poet of the Baul tradition. "Snared by the Beauty" is from *The Mirror of the Sky*, translated by Deben Bhattacharya (Prescott, Ariz.: Hohm Press, 1999), p. 85. Used with permission.

Isha Upanishad · *See* Upanishads.

Jnaneshwar (late 13th century), also known as Jnanadeva · A great poet-saint best known for his *Jnaneshvari*, a long commentary/retelling of the *Bhagavad Gita* (which he wrote as a teenager) in Marathi, the language of Maharashtra, India. "The Nectar of Self-Awareness" by Jnaneshwar is from *The Inner Treasure*, by Jonathan Star (New York: Tarcher-Putnam, 1999).

Kabir (15th century) · One of India's greatest mystics. This Muslim-born poet is revered by Hindus and Muslims alike. "The Swing of Consciousness" by Kabir is from *The Inner Treasure* by Jonathan Star (New York: Tarcher-Putnam, 1999). "The Simple Union" by Kabir is from *Songs of Kabir*, translated by Rabindranath Tagore (York Beach, Maine: Samuel Weiser Inc., 1974).

Lalan (died 1890), also known as Lalan Fakir or Lalan Shah · A celebrated Bengali poet of the Baul tradition. "Turned to Gold" by Lalan is from *The Mirror of the Sky*, translated by Deben Bhattacharya (Prescott, Ariz.: Hohm Press, 1999), p. 147. Used with permission.

Mahadeviyakka (12th century) · One of the great poet-saints of the Lingayat sect of Shiva-worshipers, she wrote in Kannada, the language of Karnataka in South India. "Show Me Your Way Out," "O Lord White As Jasmine," and "If My Head Falls from My Shoulders" by

Mahadeviyakka are taken from *Speaking of Siva*, translated by A. K. Ramanujan (Penguin Classics, 1973), copyright © A. K. Ramanujan, 1973.

Mirabai (c. 1498–1546) · A leading poet-saint of North India. Her songs of love for Lord Krishna are still sung throughout India today. "Deep into the Night" by Mirabai is from *The Inner Treasure* by Jonathan Star (New York: Tarcher-Putnam, 1999). "Money's No Good Here" is taken from *For the Love of the Dark One* by Andrew Schelling (Prescott, Ariz.: Hohm Press, 1998), p. 64. Used with permission. "Who Can Discredit Me?" is taken from *For the Love of the Dark One* by Andrew Schelling (Prescott, Ariz.: Hohm Press, 1998), p. 69. Used with permission.

Mundaka Upanishad · *See* Upanishads.

Nisargadatta Maharaj (1897–1981) · A spiritual master who lived as a modest householder in Bombay. "I Am a Child" by Nisargadatta Maharai is from *I Am That: Talks with Sri Nisargadatta Maharaj,* translated from the Marathi recordings by Maurice Frydman; edited by Sudhakar S. Dikshit. Durham, North Carolina, The Acorn Press, 1982 (11th printing 2000), p. 239. by Nisargadatta Maharaj (Durham, N.C.: The Acorn Press, 1982).

Ramakrishna (1836–1886) · Bengali spiritual master, worshiped by many as a divine incarnation. Ramakrishna embraced all the paths to God but had a special love for the Divine Mother. From *The Gospel of Sri Ramakrishna* as translated into English by Swami Nikhilananda and published by the Ramakrishna–Vivekananda Center of New York, Copyright 1942, by Swami Nikhilananda.

Ramana Maharshi (1879–1950) · This outstanding spiritual master of modern times taught a form of self-inquiry based on the question "Who am I?" All the excerpts from the teachings of Ramana Maharshi are taken from *The Collected Works of Ramana Maharshi* (Tiruvannamailai, India: Sri Ramanasraman, 1979).

Ramprasad (1718–1775) · A Bengali poet-saint whose songs of devotion to Kali, the Divine Mother, are still sung throughout Bengal today. "A Country Fair for Those Mad with Love," "Abandon Whatever Limits You Cling To," and "I Would Not Even Care to Be an Emperor" by Ramprasad are taken from *Mother of the Universe* by Lex Hixon (Wheaton, Ill.: Quest Books, 1994). "I'm Going to Plunge Anyway" by Ramprasad is taken from *Grace and Mercy in Her Wild Hair*, translated by Leonard Nathan and Clinton Kelly (Prescott, Ariz.: Hohm Press, 1999), p. 27. Used with permission. "Cut This Black Snarl" by Ramprasad is taken from *Grace and Mercy in Her Wild Hair,* translated by Leonard Nathan and Clinton Kelly (Prescott, Ariz.: Hohm Press, 1999), p. 44. Used with permission.

Rig Veda · The most ancient of the Vedic collections of hymns, considered the Hindus' most sacred scripture. "In the Beginning Love Arose," "Creature Fervor," "The Mighty Earth," and "The Man" are taken from *The Vedic Experience: Mantramanjari* by Raimundo Pannikar (Delhi: Motilal Banarsidas, 1977).

Shankaracharya (788–820 or c. 700), also known as Shankara · The greatest proponent of the nondualist philosophy known as Advaita Vedanta. "The Six Stanzas of

Salvation" by Shankaracharya is from *The Inner Treasure* by Jonathan Star (New York: Tarcher-Putnam, 1999). "In the Fire of Knowledge" from the *Vivekachudamani* of Shankaracharya is from *The Collected Works of Ramana Maharshi* (Tiruvannamailai, India: Sri Ramanasraman, 1979).

Shvetashvatara Upanishad · *See* Upanishads.

Tagore, Rabindranath (1861–1941) · The winner of the 1913 Nobel Prize for literature was a poet, novelist, playwright, philosopher, and social reformer. "The Sickbed–21" is from *Selected Poems: Rabindranath Tagore*, translated by William Radice (Penguin Books, 1985). Translations copyright © William Radice, 1985.

Taittiriya Upanishad · *See* Upanishads.

Mandukya Upanishad · *See* Upanishads.

Tukaram (1598–1650) · A great poet-saint who wrote devotional verse in Marathi, the language of Maharashtra, India. "God's Name" by Tukaram is from *The Inner Treasure* by Jonathan Star (New York: Tarcher-Putnam, 1999).

Upanishads ("sitting near") · Etymologically, the word suggests sitting at the feet of an illumined adept in an intimate session or spiritual instruction. The Upanishads are sacred scriptures that celebrate nondualism and are the wellspring of India's greatest spiritual philosophies. They are considered the final phase of the Vedic revelation and were composed between 1300 and 800 BCE. "Brahman Is Joy" and "For the Love of the Soul" are from *The Upanishads*, translated by Juan Mascaró (Penguin Classics, 1965), copyright Juan Mascaró, 1965. All other excerpts from the Upanishads are from *The Upanishads* by Eknath Easwaran, founder of the Blue Mountain Center of Meditation, copyright 1987; reprinted by permission of Nilgiri Press, Tomales, California. *www. nilgiri.org.*

Vedas ("knowledge") · The oldest sacred texts of Hinduism, believed to have originated from divine revelations received by seers of ancient India.

Vivekananda (1863–1902) · A primary disciple of Sri Ramakrishna and founder of the Ramakrishna Order. Swami Vivekananda established the Vedanta Society in New York in the 1890s. For "Worship the Living God," "All Gods Are in You," "The Supreme Worship," and "The Open Secret," from "Vedanta: Voice of Freedom" © Vedanta Society of St. Louis, 205 S. Skinker Blvd., St. Louis, MO 63105.

Yoga Vasishtha · A lengthy poem presenting Vedantic teachings in the form of a dialogue between the sage Vasishtha and his pupil, Prince Rama. "The Story of the Rock is reprinted by permission from *The Concise Yoga Vasistha* by Swami Venkatesananda, the State University of New York Press © 1984, State University of New York. All rights reserved.

Every effort has been made to contact publishers to obtain their consent for reproducing quotes requiring permission under the existing copyright law. In cases where no response has been forthcoming or where I have been unable to trace the author's or publisher's present address, I would be glad to add a full acknowledgment in future editions of this work as soon as I have been notified.